# Mind-Rain

## Other Titles in the Smart Pop Series

*Taking the Red Pill*

*Seven Seasons of Buffy*

*Five Seasons of Angel*

*What Would Sipowicz Do?*

*Stepping through the Stargate*

*The Anthology at the End of the Universe*

*Finding Serenity*

*The War of the Worlds*

*Alias Assumed*

*Navigating the Golden Compass*

*Farscape Forever!*

*Flirting with Pride and Prejudice*

*Revisiting Narnia*

*Totally Charmed*

*King Kong Is Back!*

*Mapping the World of the Sorcerer's Apprentice*

*The Unauthorized X-Men*

*The Man from Krypton*

*Welcome to Wisteria Lane*

*Star Wars on Trial*

*The Battle for Azeroth*

*Boarding the Enterprise*

*Getting Lost*

*James Bond in the 21st Century*

*So Say We All*

*Investigating CSI*

*Webslinger*

*Halo Effect*

*Neptune Noir*

*Coffee at Luke's*

*Perfectly Plum*

*Grey's Anatomy 101*

*Serenity Found*

*House Unauthorized*

*Batman Unauthorized*

*In the Hunt*

*Flirtin' with the Monster*

# Mind-Rain

## YOUR FAVORITE AUTHORS
## ON SCOTT WESTERFELD'S UGLIES SERIES

Edited and Original Introduction by Scott Westerfeld

With Leah Wilson

BENBELLA BOOKS, INC.
*Dallas, TX*

**BENBELLA**

BenBella Books, Inc.
6440 N. Central Expressway, Suite 503
Dallas, TX 75206
www.benbellabooks.com
Send feedback to feedback@benbellabooks.com

Printed in the United States of America
10 9 8 7 6 5 4 3 2 1

Library of Congress Cataloging-in-Publication Data is available for this title.
ISBN 978-1933771-34-2

Proofreading by Stacia Seaman
Cover illustration by Mondolithic Studios, Inc.
Cover design by Laura Watkins
Text design and composition by PerfecType, Nashville, TN
Printed by Bang Printing

Distributed by Perseus Distribution
perseusdistribution.com

To place orders through Perseus Distribution:
Tel: (800) 343-4499
Fax: (800) 351-5073
E-mail: orderentry@perseusbooks.com

Significant discounts for bulk sales are available. Please contact Glenn Yeffeth at
glenn@benbellabooks.com or (214) 750-3628.

# CONTENTS

**Introduction / 1**
Scott Westerfeld

**All That Glitters Is Not Hovery / 5**
Lili Wilkinson

**Best Friends for Never / 19**
Robin Wasserman

**Team Shay / 41**
Diana Peterfreund

**Two Princes / 55**
Sarah Beth Durst

**Why the Prince Bites It / 69**
Gail Sidonie Sobat

**A *Special* Hero / 83**
J. FitzGerald McCurdy

**Challenging the Gods / 93**
Rosemary Clement-Moore

**Beauty Smackdown / 109**
Janette Rallison

**Conformity by Design / 123**
Linda Gerber

**The Beautiful People / 133**
Charles Beaumont

**Liking What You See: A Documentary / 155**
Ted Chiang

**Naturally Unnatural / 197**
Will Shetterly

**The S-Word / 209**
Jennifer Lynn Barnes

**Lies and Consequences / 223**
Delia Sherman

# INTRODUCTION
## Scott Westerfeld

THERE'S AN OLD SAYING that goes like this: "It takes a village to raise a child."

This saying doesn't suggest that parents are unimportant, only that children are hungry little sponges who are shaped by everything around them. They need a lot more than the input of a nuclear family to reach their full potential—they need a community. The larger the world that a child experiences, the more they can become themselves.

Having spent the last five years emailing with, talking to, and lurking on the blogs of Uglies fans, I would humbly submit that it also takes a village to read a book.

Again, this doesn't mean we authors aren't important. We still want the last word in certain kinds of arguments. (That's why it's called *author*ity, people!) And we still crave all those fan mails and delicious royalty checks.

But books, like children, are hungry things. They want more than just one spindly author. They want fanfic and fan art and discussion boards and LJ icons cribbed from their covers. In a word, books want *conversations*.

1

Of course, you guys know this already. You write me all the time to tell in mind-bending detail how you gave the Uglies books to your best friends, who passed it on to their friends, until you had whole cafeteria tables wa-ing and la-ing and generally confusing everyone around them with bubbletalk. So clearly you know the secret of getting the whole village reading.

Because when more people read a book, *the book gets better.*

But why is that, anyway?

Well, part of it is the simple truth of humanity: we're social creatures. We need to talk about our lives, including our friends and families. So why wouldn't we want to talk about the characters and events we know from fiction? Just because they aren't real doesn't mean we can't gossip about them.

But a weird kind of magic happens thanks to all this conversation—it makes a book more real. It rewires your brain a little, nudging you over into a world where bubbletalk and hoverboards are commonplace, and where Tally Youngblood is flesh and blood.

So *this* book, the one you're holding in your hands, is a continuation of that process. It's more of that conversation. Maybe the gossip here has been refined a little (with quotes and references and footnotes!) but its main purpose is the same: to make the Uglies books a little better, and the village a little bigger.

In these pages, our contributors examine the language and slang of Tally's city; plumb the secret life of Shay; compare David with Zane as boyfriend material; look at some Tally-like heroes from myth, literature, and history; ask whether Tally is a hero at all; explore deep questions of beauty; contrast the Prettytime to Japanese culture; review the history of brain and body modification; scrutinize the science of the series; and invite you to join a history class in Aya's world.

In short, all the things you've already been doing around the cafeteria table, just more of it. Because like those little sponge-children, books always want more.

As an added bonus, we've included Ted Chiang's short story "Liking What You See" and Charles Beaumont's classic "The Beautiful People," both of which inspired me to invent Tally's world.

So thanks to all my brave contributors, who took some time off from writing their own wonderful YA to talk about mine. That's a great compliment, always. But mostly thanks to you Uglies readers out there who talk the bubbletalk, make the fan art, clog the comment threads, and generally spread the word.

Without you guys in the conversation, my job would be about one percent as fun.

# All That Glitters Is Not Hovery

## Slang, Language, and Identity

**Lili Wilkinson**

How many of you have ever said "bubbly" or "bogus" or "icy" to an uncomprehending bystander? That's right, all of you have.

And wasn't it fun?

Lili Wilkinson is here to tell you why. She thinks it's because if you're a teenager, language belongs to you. You're officially in charge of slang and poetry and song lyrics and nicknames. So it's no wonder that you'd find a set of books as slang-ridden as the Uglies series very brain-infecting.

Away we go.

*Teens are generally more interested in language than adults. They produce more slang, more poetry, more neologisms and nicknames, and memorize more song lyrics than their elders. They're still acquiring language in ways that most adults aren't: as a tool for self-definition.*
—SCOTT WESTERFELD[1]

**Shay sometimes talked in a mysterious way, like she was quoting the lyrics of some band no one else listened to. (*Uglies*)**

What if you had no control over your body? The way you looked, what you wore? How your brain worked? How would you still know that you were *you*?

When you see me, how do you know I'm me, and not someone else?

There's how I look, where I live, what I wear. What I listen to, read, watch.

And there's the way I talk.

I live in Melbourne, Australia. Here, when you blow off fifth period and go shopping, you're *wagging*. When I give someone a dirty look, I'm giving them a *greasy*. In Adelaide, 1,000 kilometres away, *wagging* is *cutting*, and *greasies* are *daggers*.

Where I live, carbonated beverages are called soft drinks, not pop or fizz or soda. We sleep under a doona, not a duvet or comforter, and eat capsicums, not bell peppers. We travel in lifts, not elevators, and the storage compartment at the back of our cars is called the boot, not the trunk.

Sometimes only a single letter is different—like the way we have maths classes and the U.S. has math classes. You wouldn't think a single letter could tell you much about a person, would you? But it does.

---

[1] Interview at slayground.livejournal.com/113442.html

These things mark me as Australian, and that's a big part of my identity. But the language I use isn't just about where I come from.

Do you write *please* or *plz* or *pls*? When you sign off an e-mail, do you say *love and other indoor sports*, or *with love and hugs* or *xxxxxxxoxoxoxo* or *kthxbai*?

All of these things shape who you are, make you different from the people around you. I can tell my dad is over fifty, because he says *groovy* and uses the phrase *surfing the net.* *cringe*

The language that Tally uses in the Uglies series is what makes her come alive. Especially the slang she uses. Westerfeld is very careful not to use current slang in his work, for fear of his books dating too quickly or trying too hard. "Slang," he says, "is like a fish. Good when it's fresh or when it's old, a fossil. But in between is a nasty period, something you don't want at all."[2]

Tally's slang is a mix of fresh-fish and fossils, bits and pieces, from the 1920s slang of Evelyn Waugh (*bogus* and the *-making* suffix, like *shy-making* and *happy-making*), to entirely new words like *surge* and *hovercam*. And some of the things she says are very familiar to me—*littlies, crumblies,* and *SpagBol* are all Australianisms.

It's a hard line to walk, the line between slang that's original—different enough to signal to the reader that this future world we're in is not like ours—and natural-sounding, like real live people use it every day.[3]

Westerfeld describes it as "slang from 20 minutes in the future from the next town over; slang that's a little bit off but hangs together."

---

[2] Interview at slayground.livejournal.com/113442.html

[3] Other times this has worked really well is the use of the word *smeg* in British comedy sci-fi *Red Dwarf*, and *frak* in *Battlestar Galactica*, which was such a successful four-letter-word that you can also find it popping up in other TV shows, like *Veronica Mars* and *Gilmore Girls*.

**"The street finds its own uses for things."**
                                                —Gibson's Law


That phrase could just have easily been "teenagers find their own uses for things." Teenagers are the masters of re-appropriation and remixing.

Two examples:

1. SMS was in mobile phones for a long time before anybody thought to use it. The telcos thought it might be useful for letting customers know they had voicemail, but didn't consider that it could be used for person-to-person communication. In 1995, the average mobile phone user sent three text messages per year. Now, 1.5 billion texts are sent each week in the U.S., and most of them by teenagers.

   Adults didn't realize the potency of SMS. The telcos didn't foresee it either. It was teenagers who recognized the potential of texting, and turned it into an industry that rakes in more than triple the returns of Hollywood.

2. In 2005, some nefarious entrepreneur came up with a great product: an ultrasonic teenager repellant to stop kids from loitering outside shops or train stations. It was basically a speaker emitting a really annoying high-pitched noise that only the fresh young ears of teenagers could detect. Nice, huh? Well, the teenagers had the last laugh—someone made an MP3 of the sound and started using it as a mobile ringtone. Suddenly teens could receive calls and texts in class without their teachers noticing.

In the Uglies world, Tally and her friends remix stuff too—they find alternate uses for bungee jackets, hoverboards, and hoverball rigs. They start fashion trends to disguise their rebellion, use vodka to melt ice and create havoc, and disguise syringes as broadcasting devices. The Sly Girls in *Extras* are also experts at hacking the system—surfing the mag-lev trains and using the mass driver to fling them up out of the mountain so they can skydive.

But these characters don't just appropriate and find uses for *things*. They also do it with *language*.

**"And then I saw your face on the newsfeeds, Tally. All wide-eyed and innocent and telling your *bubbly* little tale." (*Pretties*)**

Isn't it just totally cringe-making when adults try to use slang? Like when your Great Uncle Pete tries to talk like you? When he assures you he's a *fully sick, groovy dude?* It hurts, doesn't it?

The adults in Tally's world don't use slang. When they do, it's self-conscious, like the example above, when Dr Cable is mocking Tally.

Slang belongs to teenagers. Teenagers invent it, reinvent it, keep it fresh. It's teenagers who decide what's cool, and what is so over.

Sure, sometimes slang gets absorbed into our general language—like *cool* and *awesome*, or *littlies* and *crumblies* in Tally's world—but on the whole, it's all about the teenagers. Slang belongs to teenagers, because *teenagers love language*. And they love *playing* with language (usually much to the horror of their parents/teachers). It was teenagers who popularized text-speak and 733t. Everyone writes poetry when they're a teenager. Everyone obsessively memorizes song lyrics. Everyone writes letters and invents secret codes and funny nicknames and creative handles.

Part of the appeal of using slang is being able to have a secret language for just you and your friends. The idea of cliques is one that's very prominent in the Uglies series—from the reasonably "normal" Jocks, Crims, Twisters, and Swarmers in *Pretties* to the sheer craziness of *Extras*: Tech-heads, Manga-heads, Reputation Bombers, Pixel-skins, the NeoFoodies (who "made ice cream with liquid nitrogen, and injected flavors into weird forms of matter"), and of course the Sly Girls, and the followers of Radical Honesty, who have brain-surge to make them only speak the truth.

And all these cliques have their own bits of slang, words and sayings that make them unique. Imagine for a minute that you'd never read any of the books, and you overheard somebody say, "Tally-wa, you are so missing. Didn't you get the ping?" (*Pretties*). You'd have no idea what they were talking about. Or what about, "Bubbly is *not* bogus, lazy-face"? (*Pretties*).

Tally's journey from ugly to pretty to special and then out the other side is not just a physical journey. It's also a journey through language, as Tally takes on the slang of her various new cliques and then slowly comes to realize that when your body keeps changing, sometimes the way you speak is the only piece of *you* that you can hold on to.

At the beginning of *Uglies*, all Tally wants is to be pretty. She creates endless morphological models of what she might look like after the operation, she sneaks across the river into New Pretty Town to look at the pretties, and spends all her time thinking about being one—the clothes, the parties, the perfect faces.

Uglies' slang is . . . ugly. It's all about giving people nicknames that highlight their ugliness—*Skinny*, *Squint*. As Tally says, "Better dead than ugly."

When Tally leaves the city and visits the Smoke, she starts to reassess. Especially when she finds out the truth about being pretty—that it makes you brain-missing. But of course, as soon as Tally thinks she's chosen the clique where she belongs—the Smokies—everything goes horribly wrong and Tally is dragged back to the city, where all her dreams come true and she is finally made pretty.

But Tally doesn't make a very good pretty. She isn't docile or passive—she's a Crim.

The Crims dare to be bubbly—aware, bright, and fizzing, like champagne. Being "pretty" isn't something to aspire to anymore—*prettyheads* are docile, innocent, malleable, stupid. Like sheep. It's all about being bubbly now.

But like champagne, there's still plenty of fun in being bubbly—the awakeness that you get from being bubbly is channeled into pulling pranks, bucking the system, and partying hard.

By the time we get to *Specials*, Tally is sneering at the Crims. Now they're *bubbleheads*, like children playing at being grown-up. Now that Tally is special, she's *icy*. Where champagne is fizzy and bubbly and fun, ice is cold, hard, clear, and sharp. Being icy is not about having fun. Iciness is dangerous. There isn't much room in iciness for love, and that's where Tally gets herself into trouble.

**"I'm not sure *what* I am anymore, Zane. Sometimes I think I'm nothing but what other people have done to me—a big collection of brain-washing, surgeries and cures." She looked down at her scarred hand, the tattoos flickering brokenly across her palm. "That, and all the mistakes I've made. All the people I've disappointed." (*Specials*)**

Tally's body is constantly changing (much like a real teenager's body does)—going from ugly to pretty to Crim to special to . . . whatever she is at the end of the series. How much of Tally's body is really *hers* and not just smart plastic and ceramic bone? If even her brain is being operated on, then how does Tally stay Tally? How do we know, as readers, that it's still her in there? That she hasn't become *totally* pretty, or *totally* special?

Through her use of language. Through the things she says, the way she speaks, the slang she uses. When your brain, body, and lifestyle are in a constant state of change,[4] language is your

---

[4] Do you see what Scott did there? With Tally and all the surgery and change as a metaphor for adolescence? Isn't he clever?

only constant. Language is the way you shape and express your identity.

It's what makes Tally fall in love with Zane: "That's not why I chose you, Zane. Not because of your face. It's because of what you and I did together—how we freed ourselves" (*Specials*). When Zane is sick and Tally is a Special, she can barely stand to look at him. His fingers tremble, his eyes are watery. He isn't icy, he's . . . average. But when Tally closes her eyes and *listens* to his voice, his words, then she softens and kisses him.

David falls in love with Tally in the same way—overlooking her ugliness and seeing her beauty within. As Zane points out, David "took on five million years of evolution. He saw past your imperfect skin and asymmetry and everything else our genes select against" (*Pretties*).

David doesn't use slang. His language is completely dialect-free, and that makes him one of the most unique characters in the Uglies series. In a book where everyone is talking about whether bubbly is bogus, or whether their new surge is shame-making, or how many milli-Helens a new pretty might score, someone whose language is stripped of slang tends to stand out. And that's how we know that David was born outside the City—he's never been an ugly, and he'll never be pretty.

**"I'm honored to meet you, Tally-sama."**
**"Um, actually it's Tally *Youngblood*." (*Extras*)**

Here in Australia, *everyone* has a nickname. Redheads are called Bluey. Tall men are called Shorty. If the characters from the Uglies series were Australian, you'd have been reading about Davo, Zaney-boy, Shazza, and the Tallynator.

Teenagers are the reigning sovereigns of nicknames. Most teenagers have at least one nickname, whether it's used as a term of affection or ridicule. But what do nicknames *mean?* Why do we use them? We call our friends by nicknames to show that we are close, that we know things about them that other people don't. You call your boy/girlfriend *honey* or *darling* to tell them that you love them. Your mum probably does the same to you.

We also use nicknames to tease people, especially about their physical appearance. So people with glasses become Four-eyes, and redheads become Fantapants. And finally, we use nicknames to undermine people who are more powerful than us. Like politicians, and teachers. If you have a teacher called, say, Mr. Marsh, and he was a softie, you might call him Mr. Marshmallow. But if he was mean, you might call him Mr. Harsh.

In Tally's world, nicknames are almost as common. The whole *Tally-wa* and *Shay-la* thing is seen in its original form in *Extras*, where the Japanese system of honorifics is used.

In Japan, honorifics are attached to a person's name, in a sort of cross between how we add *Mr.* or *Ms.* in English, and the way we use nicknames to indicate familiarity, love, and respect. Except there are a whole lot of different ones in Japanese, and they go at the end of a name, not the beginning. *-San* is the one that's closest to *Mr.* or *Ms.*, and is used as a term of respect. For people who are younger than you, or close friends, you might use *-chan* for a girl or *-kun* for a boy. Hiro calls Aya *Aya-chan*, because she is his little sister. *-Sensei* is for a teacher, doctor, lawyer, politician, or other authority figure. In *Extras*, the *-sensei* honorific is used as a mark of respect toward people with very high face ranks.

Sometimes these get switched around, depending on the circumstance.[5] For example, in *Extras*, we learn:

---

[5] In real Japan, a good example is how Hello Kitty is referred to as Kitty-chan, and Winnie the Pooh as Puu-san. This is because Hello Kitty is relatively young (forty-odd years), and Pooh is nearly one hundred—and therefore deserving a higher level of respect.

Extras wanted connections with their heroes. That was
why Nana Love was always Nana-*chan*, never Nana-
sensei, no matter how famous she became. Famous
people owed the world images of themselves.

The honorific that conveys the highest level of respect is -*sama*. It's
used for people who are *much* higher status than you are. It is the
honorific you use if you are praying to a god (Kami-sama), but it's
also used by shopkeepers when addressing customers. When Aya
first meets Tally, she calls her *Tally-sama*, because Tally is the most
famous person in the world.

But Tally and her friends have their own system of adding
things onto names—Tally is *Tally-wa*, and Shay is *Shay-la*. These
are sort of nicknames, used to convey familiarity and affection,
working in a similar way to -*chan* in Japanese. There doesn't seem
to be any real difference between them, they are chosen according
to how well they fit the sound of the name.[6] But only teenagers
use them. You never hear adults referring to each other with -*wa*
or -*la*.

When Aya hears Fausto refer to Tally as *Tally-wa*, she
assumes that this is the correct title of respect for her. The first
time that Tally refers to her as *Aya-la*, Aya is "pretty sure that
-*la* was a good title. Tally had called her friend *Shay-la* at least
once" (*Extras*).

In one of those awesome examples of life-imitating-art, the
Uglies honorifics have spilled out into reality. Westerfeld typically
gets 400-plus comments on each of his blog posts, and well over
half of those comments are from fans with names like Emily-wa,
Rain-la, Shausto-la, and even Audrey-sensei. And they don't just
stay on Scott's blog, either. Fans like Haddy-la have been spotted

---

[6] When Westerfeld was in the process of writing *Extras*, he asked the readers
of his blog whether they preferred Aya-wa or Aya-la.

in the comments of Justine Larbalestier's blog, Maureen Johnson's blog, the Nerdfighters community, and Inside a Dog.

**"Don't worry, Aya-la," Tally said, firmly grasping her wrist. "You'll still be real, even with no hovercam watching." (*Extras*)**

There's a lot of talk in the media about our current "obsession with youth."[7] Our favorite celebrities are getting younger and younger—think Lindsay Lohan or Miley Cyrus. But whenever any of these young people do something stupid (which they invariably do), the adults turn into a bunch of rabid dogs at feeding time. Because our young celebrities are supposed to be these sort of perfect imaginary creatures who embody what adults distantly recall as youth. We want them to be fresh, pretty, innocent. Which basically means that while we want them to *look* like teenagers, they're not allowed to *act* like teenagers.

They should act like adults. Talk like adults. Spell like adults. *Use language* like adults.

Here's the thing. Being a young person today is a bit like being a woman was before the women's rights movement. People want to look at you, and write songs about you, and marvel at your beauty and your excellent skin. But they don't want you to have, you know, an *opinion* on anything.

Some adults will try and put you in a box and tell you that it's what you want, like how Dr. Cable and the Council make everybody *want* to be pretty, empty, and brain-damaged.

Everybody loves the pretties. They want to look at them, look after them, *be* them. When you're pretty, you don't have to worry about having a job, paying rent, going to the supermarket, or doing

---

[7] A quick Google search produced over 4 million hits.

homework. Your only job is to look pretty and have a wonderful time. What could be better?

But the thing about pretties—and the thing about teenagers—is they don't have any power.

Nobody gets to "vote in" the Council in Tally's world. They don't have elections or polls or any kind of political discourse. Because what could a pretty possibly have to contribute?

People under eighteen are not allowed to vote in the United States (and nearly everywhere else in the world). The reason given is that young people have a "lower level of reasoning." That line was also the reason given by our forefathers for why black people and women weren't allowed to vote. Also, there is no maximum voting age, but it could be argued that the very elderly often also have a "lower level of reasoning." In fact, adults are never required to prove *any* level of reasoning in order to be able to vote.

Everyone worships the pretties but they don't have any power of their own. Their identities are constructed for them—through surgery and brain lesions. The only way they can express themselves is by working *around* those constructed identities—the same way that slang is created to express things that formal language cannot. When every aspect of your life is controlled—where you live, what you eat, how you look—the only way to really express yourself is by what you say, and how you say it.

This is how Tally and her friends break free and form their own identities—by staying bubbly, staying icy, and changing formal language into slang, making it their own. The fight against Dr. Cable and the Council isn't the kind of fight that can be won with weapons. It's a battle of words and ideas. Ideas about control and homogenization versus ideas about freedom and difference.

Tally doesn't beat Dr. Cable in some all-out, action-packed battle sequence. She does it by *tricking her with words*. By convincing her that the syringe Tally holds in her hand is really a broadcasting device that has just outed Dr. Cable as the instigator behind the Diego invasion. She doesn't need hoverboards or nanos or razor-sharp teeth or a sneak-suit. She just needs one little syringe, and a whole lot of words.

Slang belongs to teenagers. *Language* belongs to teenagers. The reason why adults get so upset about text-speak and spelling "mistakes" is because they are *scared* of your power over language. They're scared you'll take it over, and they'll never be able to get it back.

Use language, play with it. It's what makes you *you*. *Enjoy* it. Invent new words and rediscover lost ones. Use them every day.

Stay bubbly. Stay icy.

---

Lili Wilkinson is the editor of the Australian teen reading Web site, insideadog.com.au. She's also the author of *Scatterheart*, *Joan of Arc*, and *The (Not Quite) Perfect Boyfriend*. She lives in Melbourne, Australia. She blogs and twitters at liliwilkinson.com.

# Best Friends for Never

## Robin Wasserman

When I'm talking to Uglies fans I often ask this question: "Who here hates Shay?" Invariably a lot of hands go up—not all, but a surprising number. Then I ask all those Shay-haters, "Can you imagine the story from Shay's point of view?" And their eyes start to cross as they remember the confidences betrayed, the disasters created, and the boyfriends stolen by . . . Tally Youngblood.

Unfortunately, I've never had time to completely rewrite the series from Shay's point of view. I think it would be eye-opening for those of you with your hands up. But Robin Wasserman's essay makes me think that someday I may just have to.

For you Shay-haters, reading what follows is going to be a bumpy ride, but trust me, it will rewire your brain in a bubbly-making way. And for those of you who always keep your hands down, it'll make you love Tally's long-suffering sidekick even more.

*This whole game is just designed to make*
*us hate ourselves.*
—SHAY, IN *UGLIES*

I AM A NATURAL born sidekick.

I say this with neither pride nor shame. It's just a fact of my life that for every time I've been the star, there have been approximately 8 million more times that I've been the planet, circling in orbit around someone else's bright flame.

Because I've been there myself, I pay closer attention than most to the girl behind the curtain. So I can admit, after close analysis, that in many ways Shay is the perfect sidekick for Tally Youngblood. In the tradition of all the greatest sidekicks (*cf.* Dr. Watson, Paris Geller, Mr. Smithers, Chewbacca), Shay's overlooked and undervalued. And no matter what Tally does, Shay forgives her. She gets mad, she gets even—and then she comes back for more. She's the wind beneath Tally's wings. She's a friend in deed to a friend in need. In good times, in bad times, Tally can always count on her, for sure, because that's what friends are—

Well, you get the idea.

Just one problem with this neat equation: Shay's not sidekick material. She obviously *thinks* she is. But Shay, who's right about so much, is wrong about this. She's not a sidekick, she's a hero.

A hero with the misfortune to be trapped in someone else's story.

## Anything You Can Do, I Can Do Better . . . Not That Anyone Cares

We've all known girls like Shay, right? She's that annoying kid on the playground, the one tagging along where she's not wanted, convinced that you're BFFs . . . and then, when you burst her little bubble with a harsh prick of reality, she's the one who rats you out to the playground monitors the first chance she gets. Shay is the girl who won't take no for an answer, the reason you have caller ID. If you're her friend, you're her property. If you're her enemy? Watch out. You know that woman scorned you're always hearing about? Her name is Shay.

Case closed, right?

Wrong. Here's the thing about Shay: All that stuff you think you know about her? It's total crap.

Because here's the *other* thing about Shay: She's awesome.

Not just awesome. More awesome than Tally. Not to mention smarter, savvier, sassier, braver, and bolder. Basically, she's Tally-er than Tally. Not that it gets her anywhere. Let's recap the events in this series, from Shay's perspective: Shay blazes a trail for Tally, right up the side of a mountain. Shay extends a hand to Tally, and helps her to the summit. Shay and Tally admire the view, for approximately thirty seconds.

Then Tally pushes Shay over the cliff.

Lather, rinse, and repeat. (And don't forget to get a little shampoo in your eyes, for that extra-fun burning sensation.)

. . . . . . . . . . . . . . . . .

Let's start with Shay's brain. Her big, bubbly brain, the one always digging for explanations in situations where other people (like, say, *Tally*) are content to kick back, munch on some SpagBol, and let the world pass them by. From the start, it's obvious that Shay is more on the ball than your average ugly. When we first meet her, she's far trickier than Tally. She knows how to hoverboard and, more importantly, knows that hoverboarding is the best route to freedom. Unlike Tally, who's content to just enjoy technology without wondering how or why it works, Shay also understands the hoverboard mechanism. She knows how to trick its safety governor; she gets that it needs iron to run and understands how that affects where you can and cannot fly.

Shay knows it all—and she shares it with Tally, setting the tone for the rest of their relationship. Again and again, Shay figures things out and then explains them to her best friend. Not just small things, like how hoverboards work, but big things, like how society works. *Shay* is the one who sees through the pretty lie, back when she and Tally are still uglies. True, she probably didn't figure it out for herself—she learned the truth from David. (This was back when David still acknowledged her existence.) But she gets points for recognizing truth when she hears it—unlike Tally, who hears everything Shay has to say, but chooses not to listen.

Similarly, Shay paves the way for Tally in Prettytown, encouraging her to be exactly the kind of bubbly Crim that Zane is looking for. Then, while Tally is off playing games with Zane, forgetting (not for the first time) that she even has a best friend, *Shay* thinks her way out of pretty-mindedness all on her own. Tally needs Zane to help her stay bubbly; Shay needs only herself. Tally says it best: "If Shay was hacking minders and scaling the Valentino tower, she was way ahead of the rest of them" (*Pretties*).

By the time they've both become specials, Tally has fallen embarrassingly far behind. It's not just that Shay is better at being a special—after all, she's had more time than Tally to get used to her new life. But her superiority doesn't stem from experience, or—as Tally assumes—a biological inclination toward special-dom. Shay is just smarter. *She's* the one who comes up with the plan to break Zane out of the city, and she's got every contingency covered. Poor, slow Tally is always one step behind. Take the Armory break-in: It's Shay's idea from start to finish. (Granted, this doesn't turn out to be for the best in the long run, but it's the only plan they've got.) As the action progresses, it's *Shay* who figures out why her city is attacking Diego, and what needs to be done to stop the war. Again and again, Shay just *knows*—and when she doesn't know, she asks.[1] Which is the smartest move of all.

. . . . . . . . . . . . . . . . .

*Okay, enough*, you may be thinking. So Shay's got a high IQ. So what? She talks a good game, but what's it all worth without a little action? A good ass-kicking's worth a thousand words, right? And maybe you think Shay couldn't kick her way through a paper wall.

Maybe your name is David. Or Zane.

"Don't tell me Shay actually rescued you," Zane says, his voice dripping with derision, when Tally reveals the real story behind the collapse of the Smoke and her return to Prettytown. How laughable, his tone says, that Shay could dream of doing such a thing!

As if Shay hadn't proven herself to be every inch the brave, independent action hero that Tally's made out to be. Let's not forget that at the beginning of *Uglies*, when Shay and Tally are both equally alone in Uglyville, missing all their friends, it's *Shay* who does something about it. Yes, Tally sneaks across the river—*once*—to see Peris. And she whines about it the entire way. Poor Tally, forced to do a trick without an adoring boy to applaud as she pulls it off. Shay, on the other hand, has been visiting Prettytown on her own for quite a while. She's got a plan—*escape*—and she's searching for a partner to help her carry it off. Tally, despite being just as lonely, spends most of her time gazing out the window, mooning about all the things she

---

[1] Now, we rarely if ever get to see Shay track down the answers she hungers for (except for the several noteworthy confrontations she has with Tally, desperate for the truth), but Shay's breadth of knowledge (about hoverboards; about the mores of the city; about the Armory, from the inside out) is proof enough that, off-screen, she's busy digging deep for answers. This is a society that depends on no one caring enough to ask questions; it's no wonder Shay always finds herself the odd man out.

wants but can't have (and this is Tally we're talking about, so it's an absurdly short list).

In the Smoke, Shay works the hardest, always choosing the nastiest jobs for herself. And once Special Circumstances arrive, Shay fights back with such tenacity that she's the first victim of the pretty operation. It's not the first time that Shay's greatest strength becomes her greatest weakness—but we'll get to that later. Because I'd hate to get distracted from the most crucial point of all, the one that none of Shay's friends and enemies can seem to remember: *Shay seeks out the Smoke on her own.*

The very thing that Tally *pretends* to do—while in reality being blackmailed by Dr. Cable—Shay actually *does*. This isn't just brave. It's the bravest act in the entire series.[2]

The Smoke proves to runaways that there's an alternative to turning pretty. Once you've seen the Smoke, you know you have a choice. After that, *making* the choice—staying—seems like the easy part. But before you've seen the Smoke, before your friends tell you what it's like, the only world you can truly rely on is the one you grew up in. Anything beyond that is a fuzzy mixture of hope and fantasy.

But with nothing more to go on than the word of some stranger she's met in the wilderness—and her own inner certainty that the pretty operation is wrong—Shay turns her back on everything she's ever known. She walks away from her life, from her new best friend, from everything certain and easy. She jumps blindfolded into the abyss, and she does it without looking back.

---

[2] Wait a minute, you say. Shay didn't flee to the Smoke because she was *brave*, she fled because she had a crush on David. And how do we know this? Because . . . well . . . *David told us so*. But outside of David's (self-serving) claims, there's no evidence that Shay was running *toward* David rather than *away* from being pretty. But David wouldn't lie, right? Well, we'll get to that sooner or later. Probably sooner.

And what does she get for her trouble?

Nothing.

Actually, worse than nothing: Her boyfriend insults her, then dumps her for her best friend—insisting it's not because he's fickle, it's because Shay sucks, while Tally's awesomeness is just too over-whelming to deny.

. . . . . . . . . . . . . . . . .

It's hard to miss the fact that Tally is awesome. After all, every charac-ter tells us so. Dr. Cable, of all people, kicks things off for us in *Uglies*:

> "But then Shay disappeared," Dr. Cable continued. "She turned out to be trickier than her friends. You taught her well."
>
> "I did?" Tally cried. "I don't know any more tricks than most uglies."
>
> "You underestimate yourself," Dr. Cable said.

Right. Except for the part where she doesn't. When it comes to Shay, Tally doesn't know more tricks, she knows fewer. But Dr. Cable has spoken. *You taught her well*, she says, and labors under this misapprehension for the rest of the series. Tally is the ringleader, the troublemaker, while Shay just goes along for the ride (perhaps towed behind Tally on the hoverboard *Shay* taught her to ride).

*Pretties* begins on a similar note: It's Shay who comes up with the idea to dress as Smokies for the costume bash, but is Zane impressed? No, because lucky Tally still has her sweater from the Smoke. You may think that owning a sweater isn't much of a character-defining quality; Zane's not so sure. "I've been waiting for someone like you for a long time," he tells Tally in their first real conversation. "At least you took the chance, Tally," he says, referring to her far-from-voluntary trip to the Smoke. "You were brave enough to find out for yourself."

True enough . . . if you replace the word "Tally" with "Shay."

Zane thinks he sees something uniquely bubbly in Tally, but in fact it's *Zane* who is bubbly—Zane who, like Shay, has the inner strength to break free of his pretty programming (though he gets some help after this from the lesion-eating nano pill). Tally allows herself to be dragged along with him, but that doesn't make her strong.

It certainly doesn't make her special.

## I Know You Are, But What Am I?

Let's say Shay really is Tally-er than Tally. That begs the obvious question: *If Shay's not a loser, why does she always lose?* True, it's possible to be awesome and still shoot yourself in the foot. Take the tortoise and the hare. Super speedy, super lazy hare takes a nap, while slow and steady tortoise inches past for the win.

Except in this case, it's more like some third party (let's call him David) knocked out the hare with a tranquilizer dart, then airlifted the tortoise to the finish line.

. . . . . . . . . . . . . . . . .

Yes, Shay has flaws. Who doesn't? But Tally has all the *same* flaws, and more—not that anyone notices.

What's that? You stole your best friend's boyfriend?

Betrayed the Smoke out of cowardice and selfishness?

Got your best friend turned into a brain-damaged pretty and your boyfriend's father killed?

No worries, Tally. Not your fault!

No matter what she does, Tally's cheering section excuses her. "Don't let Shay make you feel bad about us, Tally," Zane tells her (*Pretties*). He and David repeat this so many times, in one form or another, that they should just save time and get it tattooed across their foreheads.

But they're not content with ignoring Tally's mistakes and misdeeds. In order to fully cleanse her, all her sins must be placed on the head of some poor scapegoat.

Enter Shay.

David would have us believe that Shay only came to the Smoke because she had a sad little crush on him. But it's *Tally* who rejects her beliefs for a boy. And she does this not once, not twice, but *three* times.

She's all about turning pretty . . . until she falls for David.

She's all about *staying* pretty . . . until she falls for Zane.

She's all about being special, and devoting herself to Shay and the other Cutters . . . until it comes down to a choice between Shay and Zane. Only Shay, blinded by loyalty, could have been surprised when Tally chose the boy. The rest of us saw it coming from a mile— or at least two books—away.

Then there's the cutting. Midway through *Pretties*, Shay gets bubbly enough to escape from her pretty-minded haze. Once she realizes Tally won't help her, and that she can't replicate Tally's path to bubbliness, she decides to forge her own. Here's where things get sticky. Shay figures out that extreme experiences will make her bubbly, so she does the most extreme thing she can think of: she starts cutting herself.

When Tally witnesses this for the first time, "a shiver went through [her]." She reacts like Shay has turned into a raving lunatic: "Shay began to speak, facing upward, addressing the flag overhead like a crazy person." As the other Cutters emulate Shay, "their faces transformed to become more like Shay's: ecstatic and insane" (*Pretties*).

Now, I'm not saying this was a good plan.[3]

---

[3] I'm forced to admit that, smart as she is, Shay's plans rarely rise above mediocre, and they usually hover somewhere in the neighborhood of disastrous. Tally, on the other hand, often prefers not to make plans at all. She'd rather follow someone else's lead.

But where does Tally get off, acting like Shay's turned into some insane cult leader who's going to bring down civilization with a flick of her knife? Especially since a few pages later, Tally and Zane find themselves outside the hospital, needing to fake an injury, and so Zane punches his fist against a metal ambulance rack so hard that he breaks his knuckles. Crazy? Not as far as Tally's concerned: "For a moment, she'd thought Shay's insanity was contagious. But a wounded hand was a plausible reason for their wild ride here"(*Pretties*). (Admittedly, she's not particularly pleased a few chapters later when he wants to risk cutting *off* his hand in order to secure his freedom . . . but she never thinks he's insane.) The assumption here is that *Zane* has a reason for his self-injuring behavior—just as both Zane and Tally are justified in starving themselves. It's the only way to stay bubbly.

Which, by the way, is the only reason Shay's slicing her arm open.

Obviously, we can agree that cutting yourself is, by normal standards, capital-B Bad. Newsflash: So is starving yourself. But we're supposed to accept that Tally and Zane are just doing what they have to do. We're told that, starvation or no starvation, Tally is a hero for throwing off her pretty programming without the benefit of the nanos.

When Shay does exactly the same thing, she comes off as a psychopath. Because her cutting is somehow inherently worse, an act beyond redemption?

Or because it's Shay, so it must be suspect?

According to some people, everything Shay does is suspect.

And by some people, I mean David.

· · · · · · · · · · · · · · · ·

Full disclosure: I hate David with the passion of a thousand fiery suns all going supernova at the same time. No one is a more egregious Shay-basher. No one insults her as cavalierly, as unfairly, as gratuitously—with as little reason. By which I mean, *no* reason. But because David speaks with authority, both literal and moral, his words carry weight.

David is more than just the de facto leader of the Smoke—more, even, than the sole reason that the Smoke exists in the first place. To the refugees from Uglyville (and to the reader), he is the personal embodiment of everything the Smoke stands for. More to the point, he's an embodiment of the ideals they've chosen to embrace, at the expense of everything they've ever known or valued. David is their redeemer, a mythical figure who appeared in the Rusty Ruins, revealed a hidden truth, and led them to salvation. Everything the uglies think they know about the world, they know because *David told them.* By definition, the population of the Smoke is made up *solely* of uglies who trust that David knows best. Anyone who didn't trust David more than their parents, more than their teachers, more than the lessons they'd been taught every day of their lives, anyone who didn't believe that *David knows best*, would have just stayed home.

And because *David knows best*—because, out in the terrifyingly alien world of nature, wild-child David still holds all the knowledge and so all the power—David's renunciation of Shay is a turning point for both the book and the character. Which is why it seems appropriate to pause here and examine just how much David's behavior sucks. (The official amount would be: a lot.)

It's a character assassination in two acts.

*Act one*: David meets Tally and, like a child confronted with a shiny new toy, decides that she's The One. "You're different from the rest of them," he tells Tally, without any reason to think so. "You can see the world clearly." Tally's been in the Smoke for *less than one day* when David decides that she's a superior class of runaway. "Even

Shay, who really believes the operation is wrong, doesn't see how deadly serious the Smoke is."[4]

David goes on to confide his deep, dark secret—that he was born in the Smoke. Under normal circumstances, he'd never reveal this to someone that he's just met, but Tally's different, remember? He *senses* she can be trusted. Of course, when Shay—who actually *knows* Tally—decides that she can be trusted and leaves her directions to the Smoke, that's considered a foolish betrayal.[5] How dare Shay decide that Tally's trustworthy? Only David is qualified to make judgments like that! Oh, and maybe Tally is too, since (as far as David knows) she left a set of directions for her boyfriend. But that's okay, because Tally's different. Tally's *special*.

*Act two*: In typical guy mode, David decides he's a good guy, and good guys don't just ditch their girlfriends on a whim. Good guys have good reasons—so David invents one. He tells himself the following story: Shay sucks.

Specifically, Shay chickened out on running away to the Smoke the first time around, and thus is doomed to suck for all eternity: "I always figured she would [back out]. She just wanted to run away because her friends were." David goes on to say, "I almost told her to just forget about it, to stay in the city and become pretty" (*Uglies*).

---

[4] Just to be clear, the reason Shay doesn't see how "deadly serious" everything is—the reason no one does—is because David and his parents refuse to tell them! David knows that the pretty operation creates brain lesions, and yet he chooses to keep this information to himself. Why? Because he and his parents fear that one of the runaways might return to the city, taking the secret with them. David's solution? He reveals the secret to *someone who's already admitted she's considering a return to the city*. Smart, David. Very smart.

[5] It's true that Shay—who did make a good faith effort to introduce Tally to David—promised him she wouldn't tell anyone about the Smoke. But was she given a choice? Given the benefit of the doubt, Shay's act could even seem heroic. She broke her word to save her best friend from the pretty operation. But this is Shay. She's never met the benefit of the doubt.

And here we have the fount of my undying hatred. Thirty-seven words of total, rage-inducing crap. Let's take a closer look, shall we?

1. "She just wanted to run away because her friends were." We *know* David doesn't believe this, because a few pages earlier he admitted that Shay "really believes the operation is wrong."

2. Not that Tally bothers to mention it, but she knows—and *we* know—that Shay never wanted to be pretty. If she'd really just wanted to run away because her friends were, why cling to the idea after her friends were gone? Why not just enjoy life with her new best friend, and allow the city to make her pretty, right on schedule? And speaking of why's . . .

3. If Shay's such a pathetic follower, *why would she run away to the Smoke on her own?*

4. David's so disgusted with Shay for being a coward—yet somehow fails to notice that (according to Tally's story) *Tally* chickened out on her first chance to head for the Smoke, too. So why is Shay a coward and Tally a hero?

5. Let's say David really believes that Shay was just copying her friends (although he doesn't). Let's even say that he's right (although he's not). So what? He believes the same thing about Tally, that she only came to the Smoke to find Shay. According to David, this makes Tally a good friend. And yet, apparently, it makes Shay a weakling deserving of brain damage.

6. Another why: If David believes all this, *why date Shay in the first place?* Sure, he brushes off his relationship with Shay, acting like it's all in her head. But throughout the series, Tally and Shay refer to the fact that he was indeed Shay's boyfriend. So either Shay is completely delusional, or David's a complete asshole.

You can probably guess where I stand.

## When I'm Wrong, I Say I'm Wrong . . . Good Thing I'm Never Wrong

I don't know if you'd call it a *desirable* talent, but Shay has a special flair for holding a grudge. We're talking world-championship levels of grudge-holding. And she's certainly not shy about declaring revenge when she thinks she's been wronged.[6]

And make no mistake, she has been wronged—most of the time, by Tally.

Tally and her flock of admirers like to act like all the bad things Tally's done were beyond her control (for the good things, of course, she wins full credit). But if you examine each major accusation Shay makes against Tally, they all end up being true. Despite the fact that Tally—for all her self-flagellation—refuses to take responsibility for any of it.

*"I never meant for that to happen."*

Here Tally's referring to the theft of Shay's boyfriend—but it's basically the story of her life.[7] She pretends she had no choice when

---

[6] Although let's not overlook the fact that she rarely follows through on any of those threats—instead, grudge or not, she always throws herself into yet another doomed phase of friendship with Tally. While it's true that, in one sense, Shay carries out the ultimate revenge by making Tally a Special, it soon becomes clear that Shay sees this less as a punishment than as a reward. Shay's "betrayal" is in fact nothing but an ill-fated attempt to cement her relationship with Tally. Specials believe that everyone else is pathetic and beneath them; Shay wants to rescue Tally from this hellish life of ineptitude. "I'm sick of all the mix-ups and bad blood between us," she says, just before taking Tally down. "From now on, you and I are going to be *best friends forever*" (*Pretties*). Tally interprets this as a threat, but I would argue that in Shay's Special-twisted mind, it's a sincere and hopeful promise.

[7] Let's not forget, this isn't the only time Tally steals one of Shay's potential boyfriends. Although it's glossed over, it seems clear that Shay is nurturing a serious crush on Zane—note "Zane's praise lighting her face up like champagne." Of course, once he meets Tally, even the minimal praise he spared for Shay trickles to a stop.

it came to David: "Without even trying. She'd shafted her best friend."

Oh, really, Tally? You're so head over heels in love with the boy you've known for *two weeks* that no force in the universe, and certainly not the force of your meager self-restraint, is strong enough to keep you apart? Even though you know that you're about to break your best friend's heart?

This, not her betrayal of the Smoke to Dr. Cable, is Tally's true treason. Arguably, Dr. Cable didn't give her a choice. David did. Tally could have walked away.

She didn't.

Instead, she told herself she had no option but falling into David's arms. What's loyalty in the face of (two-week-old) love?

Tally wields the same "I didn't have a choice" stick when it comes to responding to Shay's accusations in *Pretties*. After finding out that Tally shared her lesion-curing pill with Zane rather than with her best friend, Shay freaks out. Tally can only stammer in response, "There wasn't time . . . I didn't even—"

Of course, we the reader know that Tally and Zane had to pop the pills to avoid detection; there was no time to save one for Shay. But are we meant to think that Shay's being unreasonable? That she's holding Tally to an unfair standard because she doesn't understand the situation? That yet again poor Tally has accidentally, through no fault of her own, found herself at odds with her beloved best friend?

I'm not buying it.

Tally may not have had a choice once she was on top of that tower with the pills in her hand . . . but who told her to go up there with Zane in the first place? Who told her to confide in a boy she barely knew, leaving her supposed best friend out in the cold? Tally may not have chosen Zane over Shay in that crucial moment—but she chose Zane in every moment that came before it. She had a choice; she chose the boy. She makes the same choice again in

*Specials*, choosing to follow Zane and the other Crims instead of sticking with Shay and fulfilling the mission of the Cutters. And this after Shay has risked *everything* to give Tally what she wants (i.e., Zane).

"It didn't seem fair," Tally thinks, when Shay calls her on this. "When had she even had a chance to be selfish? Ever since Dr. Cable had recruited her other people had made most of Tally's choices for her."

There's something extremely peculiar about the so-called hero of this series—a series which celebrates the triumph of personal choice and the freedom of thought—constantly asserting and embracing her lack of agency. Tally is venerated as the figure who gave people their minds back, allowing them to choose their own destinies. But Tally seems to live in a state of denial that she has any choice of her own: "And yet she and Shay always seemed to wind up on opposite sides. Was that a coincidence? Or was there something about the two of them that always turned them from friends into enemies?"

Yes, there was—and its name was Tally.

But Tally prefers to believe that, "Maybe they were like two different species—hawks and rabbits, say—and could never be allies."[8] How convenient. Because if it's true, she's not to blame. Despite all the ink spilled describing how *guilty* Tally feels for everything she's done, how much she regrets the pain she's caused, the fact is, her

---

[8] This isn't the first time that Tally has found it convenient to rely on the crutch of biological determinism. In *Pretties*, when Peris backs out on escaping the city, Tally doesn't try very hard to talk him out of it. Despite the fact that he's her (former) "best friend forever," despite the fact that he was a much trickier ugly than she was, criticizing the pretty operation in much the same way Shay used to, despite the fact that many of the characters we know and love, Zane included, back out on their first opportunity to run away, Tally just writes off Peris for good. "Maybe some people had always been prettyheads, even back before the operation had been invented. Maybe some people were happier being that way."

words are empty. *I'm sorry,* she says, over and over again, *but can you really blame me?*

*I had no choice.*

Zane backs her up—right before he loses his life, because of Tally.

David backs her up—after he loses his father, because of Tally.

Only Shay—who, not incidentally, has lost everything that matters several times over, because of Tally—calls her on the truth: "You have to stop trying to run away," she says, after it becomes clear that their raid on the Armory caused a war, "and face what we started."

. . . . . . . . . . . . . . . . .

Shay's greatest strength—along with her greatest weakness—is her inability to hide from the truth.

Tally lies about everything, to everyone. She lies to save herself (e.g., when she's spying on the Smoke for Dr. Cable), she lies by staying silent (e.g., whenever she lets one of her boys believe she's braver and stronger than she knows herself to be), and when nothing's at stake, she lies out of habit (e.g., when she's exaggerating the hardships of her journey to the Smoke). Worst of all, she lies to herself: "I kind of like being fooled about some things."

Shay, on the other hand, would rather be miserable than be fooled. In *Specials,* Tally gets nostalgic for the easy life in Prettytown. Shay's not having it: "It was bogus," she says. "I'd rather have a brain."

Tally's lies smooth her way to redemption. Her lies lead her to David, to Zane, to the wild, to freedom. But Shay takes the opposite path. It's her hatred of hypocrisy, her rigid honesty, and her demand for authenticity that allow her to break free of the system in both *Uglies* and *Pretties.* Unlike other uglies, she doesn't want a pretty face; she doesn't want to be anyone but who she is. For Shay, honesty is always better than dishonesty, even when it's ugly.

As the truth usually is.

## It Takes Two to Make a Dream Come True—But Only One to Make a Happy Ending

Seconds later, two faces appeared on the screen. Both of them were Shay, but there were obvious differences: One looked wild, slightly angry; the other had a slightly distant expression, like someone having a daydream.

—FROM *UGLIES*

When we first meet her, Shay's a reasonably happy, well-balanced character—until she collides with Tally Youngblood, who forces her to make a choice between the two sides of herself, the fighter and the dreamer.

We all know Shay's a fighter. Increasingly, over the course of the trilogy, we come to know her as embittered and aggressive, lashing out at anyone who doesn't live up to her high standards. Tally earns a reputation as a fighter as well (despite the fact that most of her battles are fought by accident); unsurprisingly, she's seen as someone who chooses the *right* fights, while Shay always finds herself in the wrong. And the more things go wrong for Shay, the harder she fights. But until it overwhelms her, Shay's defiance *defines* her, pushing her to break the rules and crack the system. "I don't want to be pretty," she tells Tally at the beginning of *Uglies*, the first time they argue. In Tally and Shay's society, you'd have to be a fighter to dredge up the courage to say these words. More than that: Only a fighter would even *think* them.

The dreamer in Shay may be less apparent, beaten down by the course of events, but we can see her in Shay's early adventures with Tally (the playfulness with which she springs the surprise of the rapids and the roller coaster gap, the proclivity for wild storytelling that leads Tally to doubt tales of David)—and, more dangerously, in Shay's perception of her new best friend. Shay idealizes Tally, as she'd idealized David before her, seeing in both of them a kindred spirit, someone who would do anything for her, repay loyalty with loyalty, ignoring any and all evidence to the contrary. The dreamer in Shay, the naïve idealist, believes in such a thing as *best friends*, and she's determined to do whatever she can to make the reality of Tally fit the mold of the fantasy.

For Shay lives in a world of ideals. It's true that she's brave to have left Uglyville and set off in search of the Smoke with no evidence that it existed, but she did have an advantage over some of her more timid friends—Shay, the dreamer, is always all too ready to believe her own stories. She tells herself fairy tales: the tale of her new, perfect best friend; the tale of a handsome prince waiting to sweep her away; the tale of a bright, shining land of possibility, where she would finally feel at home. "It's not like here, Tally," she explains dreamily early on in *Uglies*, before she knows anything about the Smoke beyond what she's been told. "They don't separate everyone, uglies from pretties, new and middle and late. And you can leave whenever you want, go anywhere you want." Shay doesn't need evidence that the Smoke exists—she has faith. She *believes* in it, just as she believes Tally will eventually join her there. Just as she repeatedly, mistakenly, believes that Tally will live up to the *dream* of Tally, the best friend who will never betray her.

But Tally does betray her, again and again, pushing Shay over the edge. Forcing her, as she forced her that day in front of the wallscreen, to *choose*.

She chooses the fight.

She fights because the world is imperfect, because it never measures up to her exacting standards—and because the deck is stacked against her from start to finish. The fight nearly destroys her, but it's also what saves her.

One could argue that Tally is able to reprogram her brain again and again because her personality is fungible. Even before the operation, she's the perfect pretty, acting without thinking, avoiding conflict at all costs, accepting whatever truth she's told. As Shay points out, she's also always been a perfect special, protecting herself at all costs, leaving destruction in her wake. Perhaps the surgeries weren't doing anything more than enhancing tendencies that she already had, making it easy to accommodate her personality to the results. The operations didn't change her so much as they just made her that much more herself. Shay, on the other hand, can't accommodate herself to anything. She's stubborn, she's rigid, and she'll never bend, only break.

Which, in the end, allows her to break free.

Still, breaking free of an oppressive system isn't enough to fix Shay's problems. She needs to break free from the anchor that's been dragging her down since day one: Tally. Technically, an injection of nanos gives Shay the happy ending she deserves. But no nano would be powerful enough to turn embittered, vengeful Shay into the happy, healthy warrior we see at the end of *Specials*. Something else must have happened.

Something did.

Midway through the story, Tally chooses Zane over the Cutters. For Shay, this is finally one betrayal too many. She walks away from the sham of a friendship, and when next we meet her in *Specials*, she's a new person. A better person.

Because of the nanos? Maybe. But not *just* the nanos. It's as if finally walking away allows Shay to unite the two halves of herself that Tally split asunder. Now she can be a fighter *and* a dreamer; she can be whole. She can be free. Once Tally's not around to force her to choose, she can choose for herself. She can tell a new story, and in this story, she's not the sidekick. She's the hero.

I don't know about you, but that's a story I'd like to read.

Robin Wasserman bears her inevitable sidekick status as a badge of honor. When not basking in reflected glory, she sits in front of her computer and tries to fill up blank pages. She's managed enough of these to make up several books, including *Skinned*, *Hacking Harvard*, and the Chasing Yesterday trilogy. They're all for teenagers, mostly because she thinks that's the best way to contribute to the mind-rain, which she believes is happening as we speak. You can find out more about her work, her life, and her assorted peculiarities at www.robinwasserman.com.

# Team Shay

## Diana Peterfreund

In this second of two essays about our mis-understood anti-heroine, we peer deeper into Shay's relationship with Tally. Diana Peterfreund vividly demonstrates how the two girls' inexo-rable bond is the engine that makes the whole series go.

This point reminds me of another question I often ask groups of Uglies fans: "Can you imag-ine these books without Shay?" Of course you can't, because without her, the whole series would be a haiku:

Later that summer,
After Peris got pretty
Tally did too. End.

And that shows you how powerful a little unre-quited love can be. And, um, how hard it is to write a good haiku.

Take it away, Diana.

"TEAM DAVID OR TEAM ZANE?" was a popular question on Westerfansites and forums (and even an Amazon Poll) during the span of the Uglies series's initial release. Readers enthusiastically debated whether Tally should be romantically linked with David, the self-sufficient, wild-born young man who first leads her into the Smoke, who teaches her how to survive in the wilderness, and who tells her the truth about her not-so-pretty world; or Zane, the charismatic, enigmatic leader of the New Pretty Town clique the Crims, the almost too "extreme" pretty who snaps Tally out of the empty-headed, pretty mindset, who is brave enough to share with her the experimental cure (though it costs him his brain), and who is willing to do anything, absolutely anything, to make up for chickening out and not leaving the city when he was still an ugly.

David or Zane? David or Zane? What love story in the Uglies trilogy is your favorite?

I for one like Shay. For me, the story of the Uglies trilogy is the story of Tally's complex, epic, often twisted relationship with her BFFrenemy. It's a tale of teamwork, sacrifice, betrayal, jealousy, double-crossing, rivalry both romantic and professional, and a few highly suspect moments of hoverboard snuggling. Shay is a driving force behind almost every one of Tally's decisions in the series, and it is because of Shay—Tally's love for Shay (and vice versa), Tally's guilt over Shay, Shay's obsession with Tally—that Tally is forced by turns to remain ugly, turn pretty, and become special.

I've had several debates with other fans of the series about exactly where on the spectrum Shay's feelings lie. Does she love Tally as a *friend*, or are there romantic implications to their rather unhealthy relationship? Usually, people deny that there's anything more to it than friendship. After all, platonic friendship and social status can be every bit as earth-shattering and important to a teenager as romantic love. Having survived the "best friend charms" battles of my own middle school experience (horrible invention; stupid broken-heart lockets, may each and every one of them rust in Hell), I'm inclined to agree that this is true. However, I think the leader of the Cutters is harboring more than just a frustrated friendship; she's nursing a broken heart.

Though Tally's pinball relationships with David and Zane are always at the forefront of the narrative, one must remember that the story is told from Tally's point of view. She may not recognize Shay's feelings—a fact that more than once sends Shay into a vengeful rage—and what's more, she may be too biased to recognize the truth of her own. While David and Zane vanish into the wilderness for months or books at a time, Shay is always there, always watching, always waiting, and always, *always* thinking about Tally.

From the beginning of their friendship, in *Uglies*, it is clear that Shay cares very deeply about what Tally thinks of her. Shay dislikes being called by her "ugly" nickname, and insists that she and Tally call one another by their true names. When Tally tries to get Shay to play the "imagine your pretty face" game so popular with uglies on the verge of their operation, Shay is disgusted. "What, can't you stand me? Do you need to get some picture in your head so you can imagine it instead of my face?" (*Uglies*). It's desperately important to Shay not only that Tally like her, but that Tally like her for who she is—not the mindless, generic, Pretty Committee–pretty she will soon become.

Tally, of course, can't understand why Shay is so worried. She doesn't recognize that Peris has become a different person since his operation, and she believes that their friendship is forever, regardless of their faces. "In less than a month she'd come to feel like [she and Shay] were best friends. Almost like how she'd met Peris as a littlie, and they'd known instantly they'd be together forever" (*Uglies*). However, at this point in the story, Tally believes that nothing counts when you are ugly. Her friendships with Peris and Shay are both preludes to the real life she thinks only begins after the operation.

After all, "when they were both pretty, there wouldn't be anything to fight about anymore" (*Uglies*). She shrugs off Shay's copious compliments on her natural face. Shay may find Tally very attractive, but the pretty biology Tally has been indoctrinated to believe trumps even the opinion of her supposed best friend.

Instead of fretting over whether or not she and Shay like each other for how they truly are, Tally spends her time not only fantasizing about her new pretty face, but also *fantasizing about Shay's*—even going so far as listing all of Shay's features, and then imagining them as they'll be once they've become the acceptable, pretty fashion. For Tally, who subscribes to the idea that only "pretty" equals right and worthy of love, her strong feelings about Shay are more acceptable if she can project them onto a pretty face. When Shay doesn't want to play the computer projection game, Tally performs the mental equivalent. Wonder what Shay would think to know that Tally is thinking about her so much?

But even her brainwashing can't overcome reality—when Tally next sees Shay, she is surprised to find that she feels her friend's ugly face is "almost perfect."[1] Her strong feelings for Shay paint beauty on her supposedly "ugly" features. A recurring theme in the trilogy is how emotion plays tricks on the so-called pretty biology that is supposed to trump everything else. The more Tally loves someone, the more she sees that their irregularities and diversions from the "ideal" are actually beautiful as well. And as Tally moves away from the city and into the wild, where irregularity rules, this tendency becomes even more pronounced.

It is only in the wild that Tally finally realizes how highly Shay values her "real" ugly identity, and despite her rejection of Shay's values, despite her intent to betray her friend, Tally admits that she "couldn't wait to see Shay" (*Uglies*).

---

[1] However, her parting shot to Shay, who has decided to run away, is that Tally wishes she could have seen what Shay would look like as a pretty.

Shay is similarly thrilled to see her, though she mistakenly believes that Tally's delay in joining the Smoke is due to a reluctance to abandon a mysterious "heartthrob" she met after Shay's departure. Shay understands, after all, she "did the same thing" (*Uglies*).[2] Shay couldn't bear to come to the Smoke without Tally, so she disobeyed her crush David and risked the existence of their outpost to bring Tally to her. Being with Tally is more important to Shay than either her conviction to remain ugly or her much-ballyhooed feelings for David.

Oddly enough, *David* seems to think Tally's feelings for Shay are more important than their own budding romance or Tally's interest in the Smoke.[3] Both before and after the Special invasion of the Smoke, he attributes all of Tally's motivations to a desire to help Shay. Poor schmuck.

After the destruction of the Smoke, Tally finds Shay again, and her long-held fantasy of a pretty Shay and her more recent desire for a Shay who forgives her have both come true—but in a way that is her worst nightmare. Shay, held captive by the Specials, is now pretty, and as she had once feared (and Tally had once hoped), the things Shay held most dear as an ugly no longer concern her.

Well, except for Tally, of course. Gone are Shay's feelings of ugly pride and anti-city rebellion. Gone is her jealousy over Tally and David and her rage over Tally's treachery—which, at the time, had caused her to "writhe like a snake in its death throes" (*Uglies*). All those "ugly" emotions have been stripped away from Shay, and what remains is only her love for Tally. The only reason she is staying in the New Smoke rather than returning to her fabulous life in New

---

[2] Though, literally, "the same thing" meant left directions to the Smoke for her "heartthrob" to find. Does that mean that Tally is Shay's heartthrob? Hmmmm.

[3] This may, in fact, be the case, though Tally's main concern is for herself. How can she get the pretty life she's wanted without her friends knowing she's betrayed them?

Pretty Town is to rescue Tally—as Shay now believes Tally tried to rescue *her*—from a life of wild ugliness. And though Tally's internal monologue is filled with guilt as the mission of "saving" her friend is thrown back in her face, she is also torn about what would help her better preserve their relationship. Tally wonders, "Which was worse: a friend with brain damage, or one who despised you?" (*Uglies*).[4]

In the end, Tally chooses to become pretty, in large part to rescue Shay from the "mindless pretty" fate that Tally is responsible for inflicting upon her. Of course, after the operation, she and Shay are in the same boat. Neither can think of a reason they shouldn't be BFFs, and they are nearly inseparable—having brunch in bed, planning parties, making sure they are pinging each other the moment they wake up in the morning.

And Tally's fascination with the pretty Shay has not faded; when her friend gets new surge, it makes Tally's heart beat faster, and she basks "in the radiance of Shay's attention" (*Pretties*). Of course, Shay has been designed that way, but even Tally admits that it's an unusual reaction to have over a person you've known since they were ugly.

Everything seems like happy-ever-after in the land of Shay-la and Tally-wa, until once again, a boy comes between them. This time it's Zane. Though it does not seem that Shay has a crush on Zane the way she did on David, she does care about his opinion. Zane is the leader of the Crims clique, and when he singles out Tally, it elevates her status in the clique beyond Shay's. But more importantly, their romance steals Tally away from Shay. Just as Tally and David formed a special bond out in the Smoke that left Shay behind, Tally dumps Shay—her BFF, the reason she agreed to become pretty and try the cure in the first place—for the new boy in her life.

For Shay, this is the final straw. Not only is Tally ignoring Shay (after Shay's devotion and hard work to get Tally into the Crims) to

---

[4] Keep wondering that, Tally, since it becomes a central question in the Zane/David ping-pong of the next book.

hang out with Zane, but she also shares with Zane the all-important brain-lesion cure she is only reminded of because of the letter to herself that *Shay* helped her write. Tally is like that friend you have that disappears every time she's got a boy in her life. Shay has every right to be mad.

The pretty operation may have clouded her anger at Tally's treachery in *Uglies*, but all it takes is one moment of clarity for Shay to remember what Tally did, and realize that her supposed best friend is no different now. Shay is not important to Tally; status is. When Shay was the coolest hoverboarder in their ugly dorms, Tally was more than happy to be her best friend. But David was the one with the cachet in the Smoke, and Zane has status in New Pretty Town. Tally is a social climber. Only Shay's love is true. "*You* are like that, Tally. You have *always* been like that. No cure is going to make you any different—you were busy betraying people a long time ago. You didn't need any operation to make you selfish and shallow and full of yourself. *You already were*" (*Pretties*).

This scene, which occurs halfway through the trilogy, is a major turning point, not only in the relationship between Tally and Shay, but in the central storyline of the series. Until this juncture, most of the major decisions Tally and Shay make are based on their love for one another. But now, Shay is motivated by one cause, and one cause only: payback. If she can't win Tally's friendship and love through devotion and care, she'll do it by force. The saying, "Hell hath no fury like a woman scorned" applies here. Shay has been discarded and betrayed by Tally. Thus all the open, genuine regard that Shay has felt for her up to this point turns right on its head with this line: "I'll remember this, I swear. No matter what sweet things I say to you, trust me, I am *not* your friend" (*Pretties*).

The next time we see Shay, she is leading the Cutters, fueled by a pain both literal and metaphorical. Maybe Tally and Shay are right, that it is physical pain or fear that makes them "bubbly." Or maybe, as Tally surmises, it could be caused by emotion instead. Tally wonders if it's her love for Zane that "cures" her. Shay comes to her realization about Tally's betrayal while hanging off the side of a tower, but it's the pain—angry, heartbroken emotional pain—that keeps her bubbly after that. Cutting herself is only an outward manifestation of her rage and despair, just as it is for those who self-mutilate in our world. Shay is cured by her love for Tally.

At the end of *Pretties*, Shay has taken Dr. Cable up on her offer to become a Special. And what's more, she has kept her threat to Tally, who recognizes Shay's "pitiless joy in having snared her old betrayer" (*Pretties*). Though she is sweet to Tally, it is a façade, just as Shay's ignorant, pretty-minded forgiveness of Tally at the end of *Uglies* was false.

Now, however, Shay knows exactly what she is doing. She tried being friends with Tally. It didn't work. This time, she wants more. She wants to possess Tally and subjugate her completely. If status is what Tally wants, if what will make Tally love Shay is status, then Shay will shove status down her throat. She will be better than David, the leader of the Smoke; better than Zane, the founder of some silly, pretty clique. Not only will Shay be a Special, but she'll also be in charge of an elite team of Specials. And on the off chance that Tally still doesn't fall into line after being dazzled by what Shay has become, well, she'll force it on her.

Just as before, when living her dream life in the Smoke was not enough for Shay unless she had Tally with her, being Special won't succeed in making Shay happy until Tally appreciates it as well. "From now on," she tells Tally, half in promise, half in threat, "you and I are going to be best friends *forever*" (*Pretties*).

Make no mistake: part of the Special operation Tally is forced to undergo at the end of *Pretties* is designed to make her subservient to her leader. And that leader is Shay. Shay has made a classic bargain with the devil in the terms of her deal with Dr. Cable. In return for

Shay's obedience to the Special Circumstances cause, she is given her heart's desire: a completely obedient, devoted Tally.

The opening of *Specials* reveals a Tally who is brainwashed into loving her new "Boss" Shay every bit as much as Shay had been pretty-minded out of her anger at Tally in the beginning of the previous novel. Tally may think her mind is clear, but her long-held fascination with Shay has reached new heights. Shay's voice now lives inside her head, care of her new skintenna, and her words are like icy fingers down Tally's spine. Shay is constantly brushing up against Tally or stroking her hair or treating her like the pet, the possession, that Tally actually is.[5] At the uglies bash, Tally is almost as hypnotized by Shay's dancing as the uglies they are trying to control are. When David kidnaps Shay, Tally's first thought is that saving her would "pay [Shay] back for all those old mistakes" Tally had made (*Specials*). Saving Shay would also impress her, which Tally longs to do, thanks to the Special brain chemistry that not only bonds her to other Specials under Shay's leadership, but also fills her with an intense loathing of being shown as anything less than Special. In short, Tally has been programmed to worship the ground Shay hoverboards over.

Once again, it seems like the two of them will be (sick, twisted) BFFs, until Tally's pesky love for Zane rears its ugly head again. Though Specials are supposed to be beyond such petty feelings as jealousy, Shay displays plenty of it every time Tally starts whining about wanting her boyfriend around. "Aren't you happy with us?" Shay asks her (*Specials*). Eventually, Shay relents, or seems to. After all, with Tally subservient to Shay's will, what could it hurt to have

---

[5] They've always had a pretty physical friendship, filled with hugs, hand-holding, and crying in each other's laps, but the sheer number of times Shay touches Tally in *Specials*, usually in an aggressive, predatory, possessive way, is eye-opening. The language is the same kind one would use to describe an abusive spouse.

Zane around as a lesser Special, as long as he can prove he's worthy? Given his brain damage, such an event seems unlikely, and Shay probably knows it. She teases Zane with the opportunity of being Special, knowing that he disgusts Tally as he is now. She also knows that Tally finds Shay fascinating and beautiful, but sees Zane as weak, childlike, and repulsive. Shay can afford to let Tally have her little fantasy, for Shay still has Tally.

Or so she thinks. As the Zane project begins to consume Tally's thoughts, Shay grows bitter. Brainwashing, more status, more opportunities, and *still* Tally doesn't love her back! Seriously, what does it take? Shay tells Tally that she'd hoped, again, that Shay's devotion to her—no matter how cruel or twisted—would change things. "It wouldn't just be about you and your latest boyfriend; I thought you might let something else matter every once in a while" (*Specials*).

One guess what "something else" Shay is thinking of. Heck, Shay was even willing to compromise and *share* Tally with Zane, indulge her with the possibility of Zane, if that's what it took: "I've been trying so hard to please you, to make this work for you," she argues to Tally (*Specials*). But the truth is that Shay is unable to accept the kind of friendship that Tally has to offer. Tally wonders if "there is something about the two of them that always turned them from friends into enemies" (*Specials*). There is. It's the fact that not only does Shay love Tally, Shay *loves* Tally, and Tally doesn't love her back.

"Just friends" is a flawed philosophy. The very fact that "just" appears in the term indicates that it is somehow a lesser state than whatever else is available. You can be friends with someone, certainly, but if you are "just friends" with them, well, usually it's because one of you wants to be "more" than friends. And that never works out.[6]

---

[6] No, seriously, it never works out. And if you think it works out, you're wrong. What you're actually referring to is a situation wherein the person who wants "more" gets over it. But then you aren't "just friends" anymore. You're friends.

The person who wants more will be jealous, will be bitter, will be angry, will be hurt—all the feelings that Shay has shown over the course of the trilogy. Sometimes, those feelings will turn whatever love they once had for the object of their desire into hatred. When Shay seeks to possess and control Tally in *Specials*, she is motivated by this scorned love.

It isn't until she realizes that not even government brainwashing is going to make Tally love her back that she is willing to set her free. Is she angry about that, too? Of course. But it's a big emotional step for Shay to take, especially given that her Special-operation brain-stripping does not exactly make her kind, or generous, or lacking in murderous rage. She's done everything both in her power and in the significant power of Dr. Cable to get Tally to choose her, and it's not going to happen. Ever. That she accepts this, given her Special brain chemistry, is even more powerful. Perhaps, just as love cured Shay and Tally's pretty-mindedness, it cured Shay's Special covetousness. After all, the only thing you can do in a situation like Shay's is *move on*.

Later, after Shay is biologically cured of the aforementioned Special-brain, even the anger dissipates. "I hate you *sometimes*, Tally. Like I've never hated anybody else before. . . . Maybe that's why I keep coming back for you" (*Specials*). You tell her! It's not Zane who saves Tally. It's not David, either. It's Shay. And unlike the previous "rescues" that the two friends have pulled off, this one is purely self-less. Shay knows by now that there's nothing in it for her.

It is at this point that Shay, having at last accepted that Tally will never love her, can finally apologize to Tally for the things that she did, and can finally let go of the promise she made Tally at the bonfire in *Pretties*. Throughout *Specials*, she has been acting like she loves Tally: caressing her, controlling her, working with her, coaching her, making her promises. But she doesn't want to force Tally's feelings anymore. When she saves Tally from the "despecializing" operation (even though Shay knows that—upcoming city-saving mission aside—Tally needs to get her brain back in order), she is finally acting like a true friend.[7] She realizes that she and Tally have no future, that Tally never understood what she meant to Shay, and that she never will.

Of course, Zane up and dies right around then, and then David re-enters the picture, and Tally is so filled with emotion about these two that she doesn't spend much time thinking about poor Shay and her unrequited love. Indeed, the first time I read the books, I spent most of my time thinking about Tally's relationships with the two boys. But as time went on, my impressions of them faded. Yes, Tally loves Zane. Yes, David introduces Tally to a whole new world. But when I think about the source of all the real passion in the trilogy, the bond that causes the most pain, the most heartache, and the most plot developments, there's only one relationship that comes to mind: Tally and Shay's.[8]

Was it platonic? On Tally's part, most definitely (despite an ongoing attraction to Shay). But Shay's behavior goes further than that of a neglected best friend. She's never happy unless Tally is around, and is deeply jealous of Tally's relationship with Zane. (Though she makes much of Tally "stealing" David from her, Shay obviously

---

[7] Tellingly, it is here that Tally finally seems to get over her three-book fascination with Shay's person. In the past, whether ugly, pretty, or special, Tally always described Shay in glowing, mesmerizing terms. The "despecialized" Shay is one that disgusts Tally as much as the crumbling Zane did.

[8] Their relationship in *Extras*, seen through this lens, is a rather sweet bit of nostalgia. Shay and Tally are both "over" their more passionate emotions—both positive and negative—and Shay's soft echo of "best friends forever" and Tally's teasing of "Boss" Shay is treated like a sentimental throwback, rather than fact. Still, even the woefully unobservant (for a reporter) Aya recognizes that there is a lot of water under their shared bridge: "You and Shay are logic-missing . . . sometimes you're like best friends, other times you seem to hate each other." One wonders if their "friendship" and civility is possible only because they see each other so very rarely.

values Tally above David, as she disobeys him and risks the secrecy of the Smoke by asking Tally to join her.) When Shay latches onto the idea that it's the status of David and Zane that attracts Tally to them, she sets about achieving her own. When even that doesn't have the intended result, she has Tally brainwashed into loving her. Shay is in love with Tally, and that love is at the root of everything else that happens. The original trilogy begins when Tally meets Shay, and ends when Tally and Shay part ways, seemingly for good. (Shay happily remains in Diego, while Tally disappears into the wild, and they don't meet again until the "emergency" in *Extras*.) Their tragic story is at the very core of the Uglies series, and its power is why I'm absolutely on Team Shay.

----

Diana Peterfreund is the author of the Secret Society Girl series, as well as *Rampant*, a young adult fantasy about killer unicorns. She first found *Uglies* when the cover called to her across a crowded Barnes & Noble, and shortly after, devoured everything else Scott Westerfeld had written. A graduate of Yale University, she lives in Washington, D.C., with her husband and her dog, writes full time, and wonders when Scott's next book is coming out. You can read more about her at http://dianapeterfreund.com.

# Two Princes

## Sarah Beth Durst

Here's yet another question I enjoy asking assembled Uglies fans: Team David or Team Zane? Hands please.

Usually when I ask this question, the number of votes for each of Tally's boyfriends is about the same. This makes my writer-brain very happy. After all, I set out to make Tally's dilemma a *real* choice, one that she could argue about in her own head for a few hundred pages, and that readers could argue about long after they closed the books. I wanted a triangle that even *I* didn't know how to square. (Which is why I sort of, um, cheated. Sorry, Zane!)

Luckily, Sarah Beth Durst is here to solve the equation. Using proven scientific techniques developed by glossy fashion magazines, she takes us step by step through the data about who's the best boy for Tally. But you'll probably want to keep score on your own, just to check her math.

Pencils ready.

*"How lucky is that?" Tally muttered to herself. "Sleeping Beauty with two*
*princes. What was she supposed to do? Choose between David and Zane?"*
—Pretties

## DAVID OR ZANE?

Who would you choose?

Who should Tally have chosen?

I think that one of the most awesome things about Scott Wester-feld's Uglies series is that it's not obvious which guy is best for Tally. Okay, yeah, in the end, Tally's best choice is the not-dead guy, but ignoring that tiny detail. . . . Both are decent guys. Both care about her, and she cares about both of them. And they like each other. It's a true love triangle. Seriously bubbly.

But one of them must be her true Prince Charming, right? So which one? I have been giving this a lot of thought, and I've decided that the best way to judge them is to subject them both to the indignities of a boyfriend quiz, like the kind that Tally could have found in one of those Rusty magazines. . . .

## Q: Is he a good kisser?

You might think this is a shallow question. . . .

Fine, it is a shallow question. But kissing is important in the Uglies series. And fun. But mostly important. You could even say it changes the world. It certainly changes Tally.

She kisses David first, and the kiss rocks her world. Before the kiss, she knew her future: betray the Smoke, rescue Shay, become pretty, and party-party-party. After the kiss, she tosses Dr. Cable's pendant in the fire. With this act, she rejects her future as a pretty, and she deliberately destroys her route home. Yes, it backfires. Destroying the pendant activates the tracking beacon, which leads to the destruction of her new home, a serious blow to her relationship with David, a mortal blow to her friendship with Shay, and eventually to the death of David's father . . . so all in all, it's kind of a bad move. But her intention is to leave her old life behind and live with David forever in the wild—all inspired by a single kiss.

David's kiss undoes years' worth of brainwashing. For the first time, it occurs to Tally that you don't have to be pretty to have a full life. As she puts it, "Uglies did kiss each other, and a lot more, but it always felt as if nothing counted until you were a pretty. But this counted" (*Uglies*). His kiss makes her feel like a pretty without a lobotomizing operation. Impressive lip power.

Of course, it's not like "I want to be pretty . . . SMOOCH!. . . . I want to be ugly!" She begins to question her future from the moment she realizes that betraying the Smoke would mean destroying David's life. Of course, she questions even more when she learns that becoming pretty means becoming brain-damaged, and that big "soylent-green-is-people" kind of revelation contributes to her decision . . . but the kiss is the true pivotal moment. She even acknowledges this herself later: "Her reality had been transformed by those two weeks in the Smoke, starting . . . when? That first time David and she had kissed" (*Pretties*).

Kissing Zane is also transformative. At the start of *Pretties*, Tally has no memory of David, and her memories of life before the pretty operation are flawed (she doesn't know she was forced to undergo the operation, she doesn't know she meant to betray the Smoke and then changed her mind, etc.). When Tally kisses Zane, she wins back several key memories. In fact, when she kisses him, she whispers David's name.

Traditionally, the girl whispering another guy's name isn't a ringing endorsement for a guy's smooching skills. But in this case, it's a compliment. Seriously. It signals the restoration of several damaged brain cells.

Kissing Zane turns out to be a more effective cure for the brain lesions than anything else Tally tries, including calorie-purging pills and death-defying stunts. She uses kissing Zane to heal her mind. So I'm thinking that despite the whisper-another-guy's-name thing . . . if your kiss has the power to heal brain damage, then you must be a pretty good smoocher too.

So I call this one a tie—a point for each set of super-lips.

Score: David = 1; Zane = 1.

## Q: Are you attracted to him?

Tally's first opinion of David is that he's an ugly. His forehead is too high, and he has a scar through his eyebrow and a crooked smile. But it's a nice smile. She notices that right away. She also notices that he carries himself with a level of confidence she's never seen before, and she wonders "how much of being ugly was just an awkward age" (Uglies). She doesn't dwell on this thought, but it's an important moment: she's intrigued by him despite his ugliness. She begins to question whether ugly is really ugly and whether it's necessary to become pretty. It's the start of her first transformation in the series.

True, we're not talking a love-at-first-sight moment here. She doesn't instantly recognize him as her Prince Charming. But does that disqualify him? Cinderella, Sleeping Beauty, and Snow White all claim to have known their princes from the first moment, but when you think about it, Cinderella went on a single blind date (where they didn't even talk enough to exchange names), Sleeping Beauty napped through her intro, and Snow White was dead. I think it's enough that Tally's first sight of David catches her attention and causes her to think; she's at least intellectually attracted to him. Later, she decides to change the course of her entire life because of him. She decides the operation isn't necessary, and she even begins to see him the same way she would a pretty.

Unfortunately for David, this attraction to him doesn't last. She's reconditioned, as part of the pretty operation, to see him as an ugly again. But it's more than that: in their time apart, she's lived through different experiences. She's been changed, and she's changed herself. She's not the same person she was the last time they saw each other, and so she sees him differently: "His face sent a shock through her. Not because he was hideous—he wasn't—but because he was simply . . . unimpressive. Not an ugly prince. Just ugly" (*Pretties*). He isn't her dream prince anymore. This doesn't mean that he wasn't her prince once upon a time, and in fact, he does grow on her again, and she regrets her initial reaction to the sight of his face as her old memories return.

When she's forced through her second operation, she doesn't lose her old memories, but she does lose her old interpretation of those memories. She again views David as an ugly or a "random." Worse, she isn't simply not-attracted to him; she actively sees him as her enemy. But by the end, she rewires herself, and this time, she learns to see him even more clearly; she sees him not as an ugly or even a pretty and not as her prince but as a person—which is arguably the best way to see him of all. "He wasn't an ugly anymore; to her he was just David" (*Specials*).

Her attraction to Zane undergoes a similar swing. Initially, she finds him to be dizzyingly gorgeous. He has shimmering gold eyes and lovely sculpted cheekbones. (For the record, he doesn't sound like my type at all. He sounds a bit like an anime caricature. But we're talking about how Tally sees him here.) At first, she's 100 percent attracted to him, and she specifically loves how vulnerable he looks when he sleeps. But later, in *Specials*, after her second round of brain surgery, she is repulsed by him. He's still beautiful, but he seems sleepy and slow to her—she's been programmed to think anyone who isn't special is inferior.

Worse, because of his brain damage, he's lost some motor control, and he trembles. This repulses her newly reconditioned brain so much that at first she can't bear to look directly at him. With time, she begins to overcome her revulsion. When they kiss again, she nearly succeeds in seeing him the way she used to. She doesn't, of course. She vomits and jumps off a cliff, which is really the ultimate way to say "I'm not attracted to you."

So at various times, she is attracted to and revolted by both David and Zane. Granted, most of the swings in her perception are due to the whole brain damage thing. Poor Tally. Every time she's happy with a guy, Dr. Cable messes with her brain so that she thinks he's unbearable. It's really no wonder she has relationship problems, but that doesn't change the fact that we have a second tie.

Score: David = 2; Zane = 2.

## Q: Would you bring him home to meet your family? Have you met his?

Yay! An easy one! Zane never mentions his parents. But David . . . David introduces Tally to his in one of the most important scenes in *Uglies*. Meeting Maddy and Az is a huge deal since they're major fugitives and reveal all sorts of dangerous secrets that Special Circumstances would like to keep suppressed. Go David!

To be fair, the parent-child relationship is different for city kids than it is for David. Tally's parents aren't part of her life, and I'm sure Zane's aren't part of his either. They don't live together. They don't even look like each other. (Tally is shocked to see that David resembles his parents; the pretty operation erases most genetic similarities.) So it just wouldn't be meaningful for Zane to introduce Tally to his folks, or for Tally to introduce either boyfriend to hers. In fact, it would probably be kind of boring. Lots of vapid smiles and pleasantries. And cucumber sandwiches. I picture middle-pretties as serving lots of cucumber sandwiches (no offense meant to cucumber-lovers).

Still, I think David still gets the win here for the parent-introduction. After all, he doesn't introduce just anyone. He didn't even introduce Shay. Just because later Tally is kind of responsible for David's father's death and his mother sort of hates her for that . . . that doesn't diminish the coolness of the introduction.

Score: David = 3; Zane = 2.

## Q: Does your best friend like him?

Heh. Yeah. Let's talk about Shay.

Shay *really* likes David at first. Worse, Tally knows this. In her first scene with David, she sees him touch Shay's shoulder, and she remembers how Shay used to talk "dreamily" about David. She suspects that Shay's feelings for David were at least part of the reason that Shay ran away before her pretty operation.

In truth, Shay and David don't have that close a relationship. As Shay points out, he never gave her gloves like he did Tally, and as Tally notices, he never introduced Shay to his parents like he did Tally. But still . . . you don't hook up with your best friend's guy or even your best friend's wish-he-was-her-guy. You just don't. Not if you want the friendship to survive. Maybe, *maybe,* it's all right if the friend says, "You can have him for I am incredibly emotionally mature and capable of withstanding a myriad of embarrassing social moments." But Shay is about as emotionally mature as my cat. (I adore my cat, but her favorite pastime is to roll onto her back as if she's inviting you to pet her fuzzy belly and then attempt to gnaw your hand off at the wrist. Shay's a little like that.) So given all that happens and Shay's personality, it's not really a surprise that Shay despises David by book three.

Shay has similar issues with Zane. She likes him fine before he meets Tally, even admires him. But once Tally and Zane start acting all couply, she resents their closeness—especially since their closeness excludes her. She resents how inseparable they are, and she *really* resents that Tally split the cure with him instead of her. And once Shay begins to feel resentment, the knives come out. Literally. In *Pretties*, Shay's resentment of Zane leads her to cut herself, establish a happy troupe of people who cut themselves, become a weaponized human, and force Tally to undergo even more brain surgery. I think it's safe to say that boys just aren't good for Tally's friendship with Shay. Of course, the fact that Shay is also a bit psychotic probably doesn't help either. . . .

To be fair, Shay does approve of Zane enough in *Specials* to help Tally try and cure him . . . up to a point. Shay's tolerance lasts only until Tally chooses to defy Shay's orders by staying with Zane rather than using the position finder to locate the Smoke with Shay. David, on the other hand, she sees as a "random." On these grounds, I think Zane has a slight edge—let's say half a point. Shay hates him a little less.

Score: David = 3; Zane = 2.5.

## Q: Are you honest with each other?

Yeah, not so much.

Tally lies to David. A lot. His initial attraction to her and their growing relationship is, she believes, built on a lie: "But the magic was all based on lies. She didn't deserve the look in David's eyes" (*Uglies*).

David does guess a fair amount of the truth. He doesn't guess about Special Circumstances, and he doesn't suspect that she came to the Smoke to betray his home, his family, and all his friends. But he does see through the stories she first tells: "Looks like you had more adventures than you're telling us" (*Uglies*). Also, he guesses that she didn't come to join the Smoke but came because of her friend Shay. But even if he'd guessed the full truth, that wouldn't change the fact that Tally intentionally lies to him.

And she continues to lie to him, even after Special Circumstances attacks the Smoke: "She'd already lost Peris, Shay, and her new home. She couldn't bear to lose David as well" (*Uglies*). She only tells the truth when Maddy, David's mother, forces her to.

As for David . . . he is always honest with her. In fact, he's more honest with her than he is with anyone else. He shares with her the fact that he isn't a runaway. He even shares his parents' secrets with her and insists that his parents explain the truth about the pretty operation.

With Zane, Tally is the one who is honest. As soon as her memories return, she tells Zane how she'd planned to betray the Smoke and how she accidentally did betray the Smoke and all the damage that caused. Later, she describes Zane as "the one person in her life she had never betrayed" (*Pretties*).

Zane, though, is not 100 percent honest with Tally. He lies to her about the severity of his illness. She doesn't realize until late in *Pretties* how much he suffered from the nanos and how much he hid it from her: "She let her eyes close, realizing at last how hard Zane must have worked to hide what was happening to him" (*Pretties*).

So each couple has one person who lies and another who tells the truth. This should be a tie, but that doesn't seem entirely fair. Zane's lie is kind of a little white lie, especially in comparison. Tally lies about planning to destroy David's life, while Zane says he feels fine when he doesn't. Zane's lie doesn't carry the kind of consequences that Tally's lie does. So I'd like to give Zane another half-point, which brings us back to a tie.

Score: David = 3; Zane = 3.

## Q: Does he like you for who you are, or does he try to change you?

Final question. Winner takes all.

Let's start with David. He likes Tally for who she is. True, in

*Uglies*, he doesn't know all the facts about who she is. He doesn't know that she's come to the Smoke under false pretenses. He has no idea that her original plan was to betray the Smoke and destroy his life (see above on "honesty"). Tally thinks that if he knew this, he wouldn't admire her so much.

Well, she might have a point there.

But really, the things that he admires about her aren't the facts of her journey to the Smoke; he admires her for who she is. Look at what he gives as the reason for why he was first interested in her: the scratches on her face. "It was a sign that you'd been in an adventure, Tally, that you'd bashed your way across the wild to get here. To me, it was a sign that you had a good story to tell" (*Uglies*). She replies that the scratches were from hoverboarding, but he's undeterred. To him, the scratches still mean that she takes risks, and he likes that about her. And he's right: she *is* a risk-taker. Seriously, the girl is constantly leaping off things. Give her something up high, and she'll invariably hurl herself off it.

She's not like the other city kids that David has met. "You're different from the rest of them. You can see the world clearly, even if you did grow up spoiled," he says. "That's why you're beautiful, Tally" (*Uglies*). This is a major moment for Tally. (When I was marking up the book for this essay, I stuck two Post-It flags to this page!) David sees her as beautiful as she is, because of who she is inside. For the first time, she begins to think that perhaps it's enough to simply be herself. Maybe she doesn't need to be pretty. Later, in *Specials*, she pinpoints this moment as the first time she switched sides, "the moment that Tally's whole world had started to unravel." See, even the protagonist thinks it was a two Post-It moment.

Despite all the physical and mental changes that Tally is forced to undergo throughout the series, David continues to look for and see the real Tally. When he sees her as a pretty for the first time in *Pretties*, he isn't stunned by her overwhelming beauty. He is speechless because he is working to see the real Tally underneath the physical changes. Once they hoverboard together, he succeeds and is able to see her as herself again. It's kind of an extreme case of what happens when you see someone that you haven't seen for years. At first, they look like a stranger. But after a little bit of time, your brain starts to pick out the features that you associate most with that person. You remember how to see them the way that you used to, and they look familiar again. David is particularly good at this with Tally. At the end of *Specials*, "He peered into her eyes for a long moment, then sighed and shook his head. 'You just look like Tally to me.'" Yeah, I stuck two Post-Its on this page too.

David's ability to see her for herself is essential to Tally's development. In the beginning of the series, it helps Tally embrace who she is. At the end, it helps Tally confirm who she is. He demonstrates to her that she is still herself despite all that's been done to her. She's succeeded in finding herself again. In those moments, David gives Tally what she needs. He says exactly the right thing at the right time, and he makes it okay for Tally to be who she is. I think that's a clear Prince Charming move.

But before we leap to any conclusions, let's look at Zane. David might cause Tally to change by what he says and does, but he doesn't deliberately set out to change her. In fact, in *Uglies*, he has no idea that he is changing her. Zane, on the other hand, continually pushes Tally to change. He likes her *because* she's someone who can change. As they search for Valentino 317 in *Pretties*, he says, "I've been waiting for someone like you." He's been waiting for someone who he can take risks with, change with, and cure himself with. And he found that someone in Tally.

Zane has tried to find someone like Tally before. He's certain that kissing someone new stimulates brain activity—he's so certain that Tally suspects prior experimentation. Not that this should disqualify him as Tally's Prince Charming. After all, he doesn't choose those other girls; he chooses Tally. She's the one that he pushes to take calorie-purging pills because, he says, hunger sharpens the mind. (For the record, it doesn't sharpen my mind. When I'm hungry, all I think is "food, food, food" like the dog in that fake-bacon commercial. But hey, if it works for them, great.) Together, they half-starve themselves, kiss, and perform death-defying stunts to stay bubbly.

Tally loves this about Zane. She loves that he pushes her and that they become bubbly together. "Whatever Shay thought, Zane had been the right person to share the cure with. He had kept her bubbly, pushing her to pass the Smokies' tests, pressing her to dare the unproven pills. Tally had found more than a cure for pretty-headedness that day—she'd found someone to move forward with, past everything that had gone wrong last summer" (*Pretties*). That says it all right there. Zane is what Tally needs at that point in her life.

He continues to push her even when she doesn't think she wants to be pushed. In *Specials*, he tells her she can rewire herself. He makes her question why she feels the need to cut herself. Later, she resists the need to cut herself by remembering the expression on Zane's face. Inspired by Zane's wish for her to change, she does change.

While David may love her for who she is, Zane is the one who makes it possible for her to *be* who she is. He helps her conquer the brain damage. That's why she chooses him to be her Prince Charming: she wants to change. She *needs* to change.

And that's why Zane dies.

From a plot standpoint, his death is an accident. He doesn't intend to die for Tally. He doesn't even know that's what he's done—he wasn't conscious for his final moments. But from a character development standpoint, that's the result: Zane's death pushes Tally to finish rewiring herself.

His death is the cost of not rewiring herself sooner. His death is the cost of the special operation, the final proof that Dr. Cable is wrong. Tally blames herself for his death, and that guilt spurs her on to fix what she and Shay have damaged, to finish rewiring herself, and to resist any further attempts others make to change her against her will. With his death, Zane completes his primary purpose: to change Tally.

So who wins here? David likes her for who she is; Zane tries to change her. Which is better?

Ann Landers would most likely say to choose the one who likes you for who you are. But then Ann Landers doesn't live in a world with rampant government-inflicted brain damage. So here's what I think: it depends on when. Tally needs different things from a boyfriend at different points in her life.

In the beginning of *Uglies*, Tally is herself without any operations. At this point, she needs David because he helps her see herself for who she is. In *Pretties* and *Specials*, she's suffered severe brain damage, and she needs Zane to help her overcome it. At the end of the trilogy, she has found herself and what she needs is someone to help her stay herself, and that person is David. So that's why I think she made the right choice in Pretties when she chooses Zane, but I also think it's right that she ends up with David—and not merely because he's the only one of the two left alive.

So our final score is tied: David = 4; Zane = 4. Both are decent guys. Both genuinely care for Tally. Both affect and change her in their own way. Both share themselves with her and have real relationships with her.

## Q: So who is Tally's true prince: David or Zane?

Both. Sometimes you need two princes.

Sarah Beth Durst is the author of *Into the Wild* and *Out of the Wild*, fantasy adventures about fairy tale characters who escaped from the fairy tale and what happens when the fairy tale wants its characters back. Her latest book, *Ice* (coming out in fall 2009), is a modern Arctic fantasy about a polar bear, true love, and one girl's impossible quest across the frozen North. Sarah has been writing fantasy stories since she was ten years old and thinks it is ridiculously bubbly and happy-making that she now gets to do it for a living. She lives in Stony Brook, New York, with her husband, her daughter, and her ill-mannered cat. For more about Sarah, visit her online at www. sarahbethdurst.com.

# Why the Prince Bites It

## Gail Sidonie Sobat

Tally Youngblood is on a first-name basis with gravity. Not that it's her fault; it's kind of a habit of mine. Whenever the story slows down, Tally jumps off something, or falls or is thrown, if not catapulted by a hoverboard into the enemy camp. She doesn't seem to mind, though, and it certainly is fun to write all those falling scenes.

But is that all it is? A quick plot-booster? Gail Sidonie Sobat doesn't think so.

Join her for a journey alongside the heroes and heroines of legend, the protagonists of humanity's oldest stories. She asks what their mythic quests share in common with Tally's travels, and how the archetypes of princes, towers, and kisses can tell us about the Uglies series.

It's an essay that will make you wonder: What if Rapunzel had had a bungee jacket?

AND GAZING DOWN AT HER, handsome Prince Charming bent to kiss her lips. Then he swooped her into his strong arms and up onto his shining white steed. They galloped toward his stalwart castle, towers gleaming in the orange rays of the sunset. And she lived happily ever after.

Puke.

As if.

Yes, it is a fairy tale. But honestly. Such endings are the wistful wish-fulfillment fantasies of erstwhile dreamy peasant girls—nowadays dreamy new-millennium girls raised on Disney pap and false promises. All that's missing are the dancing, singing mice and teapot.

Think of the fairy tales you know. The popular gooey ones. And look at the vapid girls who inhabit these tales. Girls without much backbone. Girls who mainly sit pretty, and let the men do the saving and liberating.

Cinderella, who has no more gumption than to be sweet and dress prettily and be home on time. *She* is rescued by the prince.

Cindy's close cousin, Rapunzel, trapped in a tower. *Her* great escapade: to drop her luxurious long hair down. It's the prince who does all climbing and, even after he's blinded by the witch's treachery, he is still responsible for the final rescue and transport to a happily-ever-after castle.

Sleeping Beauty? Please. *She* sleeps daintily through it all while one hundred years' worth of courageous and daring dudes try to rouse her from slumber. Yet again, it's a prince who eventually slashes through the brambles to awaken the comatose heroine.

Remember the story of Rumplestiltskin? Interestingly, the lovely miller's daughter doesn't even warrant a name. It's the creepy little stalker guy who is the major named actor, spinning straw into gold. The girl's reaction to her trial consists mainly of weeping and sniveling. *She* does almost nothing for herself. Luck and happenstance and a faithful male messenger save her in the Grimms' version of the fairy tale.

And then there's that translucent beauty, Snow White, who runs through the forest to escape her stepmother, which almost qualifies as an adventure. But then what does she do? The silly nit moves in with seven men and takes up washing and cooking and cleaning for them! When *she* succumbs to the poisoned apple, predictably, it's a face-sucking prince who saves her.

Each of these feeble, if fetching, femmes needs saving and is "holding out for a hero till the end of the night."[1] Borrrrring! Give me a real heroine with agency and derring-do and moxie, any day. Give me Gretel who saves her beloved brother! Give me Beauty who saves her beast! Give me the chick from "East of the Sun and West of the Moon."

Give me Tally from Scott Westerfeld's Uglies series.

## Tally Youngblood, Heroine

Talk about chutzpah! Guts! Cunning! Daring! Talk about these, and you're talking about bad girl Tally Youngblood. After all, good girls seldom make it into history books or the best fairy tales because mainly the boys get all the fun of saving and fighting and spitting. And that is what the Uglies series is: a kind of displaced fairy tale. At the heart of the fairy or folk tale are curiosity and awakening. Accordingly, *Uglies, Pretties,* and *Specials* explore Tally's incessant need to know the truth and her subsequent self-discovery. But a passive player she is not. Blood runs wild and fierce in Tally Youngblood. Never one to sit idly by and watch others—particularly males—do the acting or the dragon-slaying, she comes to rely on her wits, her guiles, her athleticism, her ridiculous love of thrill and danger, in order to subvert the system so tightly in the grip of

---

[1] In the words of Jim Steinman and Dean Pitchford's "Holding Out for a Hero," featured in *Shrek 2* as sung by Frou Frou and Jennifer Saunders a.k.a. the Fairy Godmother.

Special Circumstances and the evil Dr. Cable. Quite simply, Tally Youngblood gets the tough stuff done—and with aplomb!

Tally's life is a series of dizzy-making tricks, escapades, and narrow escapes; the Uglies series is nothing if not a heart-stopping, bubbly-making succession of one near-death experience after another. Witness the opening of the first three books. From the first moments of *Uglies*, under cat-vomit-colored skies, Tally Youngblood is up to tricks, crawling out her Uglyville dorm window, sneaking over to the old bridge, "hanging upside down, hands and knees clutching the knots along the rope" until she gains the framework to steal across to New Pretty Town. In *Pretties*, though a confirmed bubblehead, Tally immediately commences scheming to attend the costume party as a Smokey, "because Tally Youngblood [is] a natural Crim," already up to her old criminal ploys. Finally, in *Specials*, from the very get-go Tally the Cutter, keener and meaner, appears in full throttle on her special hoverboard, crashing the Uglyville bash, and soon after is in hot airborne pursuit of a Smokey infiltrator and David. The number of her ruses and daring episodes could fill an entire separate article.

Good girls don't, but Tally does.

After all, she is a bonafide heroine. And a tricky one, who prevails over almost anything.

Of what particularly heroic mettle is our heroine composed? A sense of justice? Check. Strength and endurance? Check. Intelligence? In spades. Risk-taking? Très formidable. Self-sacrifice? Hell, yeah. That extra something special X-factor? Well, would there even be a series if Tally weren't special? Would there be a third book at all? Even Shay herself tells Tally to "'Face it . . . you're Special'" (*Pretties*).

From bungee jacket thievery and jumping, solo-piloting to the Smoke, evading the Special Circumstances attack, and infiltrating the Special Circumstances building and diving into the elevator shaft to rescue the imprisoned Smokies in *Uglies*, to wildly leaping from the roof of Valentino Mansion, climbing the transmission tower for a key, collapsing an entire skating rink, and leaping from an air balloon in *Pretties,* to warp-speeding on her hoverboard, saving Shay from the river, breaking into and destroying the armory, leaping from a cliff (twice), hitching a ride on an helicopter, breaking free from the operating room in Diego hospital, protecting Diego from the attack of Special Circumstances, to her final escape from New Pretty Town in *Specials,* Tally Youngblood more than fulfills the criteria for taking action and being brave, if somewhat reckless. Westerfeld has created a female protagonist with a bad-ass rep who matches any hero in athletic prowess, energy, drive, and pure pluck. And like most heroes, our gutsy girl has an appetite for adventure.

## The Heroine's Journey

Adventure, usually involving danger and travel, is an integral part of the hero's/heroine's journey, a pattern common to so many stories from cultures worldwide and identified by Joseph Campbell with a little help from analytical psychoanalyst Carl Gustav Jung. Basically, the he-man or she-woman of the tale begins at home, is called to adventure in the form of a quest (often against his/her will), and undergoes a period of testing and initiation, which necessitates a descent to the underworld. This underworld—a dark, scary place like the deep Smokey woods or a bat cave or Davy Jones's Locker or the belly of a whale—symbolizes the unconscious, that place of dream and wildness where, according to Jung, one battles the fears that haunt us all, be they dragons or shadows or repressed memories and trauma. True heroes and heroines triumph over these monsters and make the return journey home, with the treasure of new knowledge (and perhaps with a golden fleece or a golden egg or two) in hand to share with the community and/or loved ones. The hero's/heroine's journey is ancient, reaching back even further than those Greek guys and grrrls to the very beginning of recorded stories. And joining the pantheon of brave heroes and heroines before her is Tally Youngblood who has definitely caught the questing fever.

That Tally is pulled unwillingly into her quest is obvious from the first book. Tally wants to be pretty. Her sole ambition is to rejoin Peris and live HEA (that's Happily Ever After) in New Pretty Town, blissful and ignorant and unconscious. Enter Shay. Catalyst. Helper figure and frenemy forever (or HFFF). She is an essential hiccup in Tally's dreams and the reason for Tally's reluctant journey. Especially when Dr. Cable enters the picture to propel Tally unhappily and unprettily forward. So the quest begins.

And like all quests, it's not about finding Shay. Not really. It's also not about meeting the prince(s). The quest is really and always about the heroine discovering herself. A journey from innocence to experience, from sleeping to awakening. A journey that a heroine—whether ugly, bootilicious, or part-android—must only and ever face alone.

## Descent into the Underworld

Perhaps most interesting about Tally's journey are the number of falls she endures. In the three books, I counted twenty-four such tumbles. By her own admission, it seems as though "her life was a series of falls from ever-greater heights" (*Pretties*). Knowing what I know about falls, I took note. To fall means to descend, usually to the underworld or to the unconscious, that important part of the heroine's journey mentioned above. To fall also implies fallibility. At the very least, a fall signifies falling from innocence. And in most instances, when Tally topples, she learns something significant.

The something significant is ultimately how to be herself, by herself. Two important questions that characters in literature seek to answer (and likewise invite us to ask ourselves) are *who am I?* and *where do I belong?* otherwise known as individuation and socialization. Throughout the Uglies series, Tally learns to "tally up" who she is and what she is meant to do. In a sense, she has to fall, "pick herself up, dust herself off, and start all over again,"[2] in order to rise.

Consider all she gains from her leaps and spills:

In *Uglies*, Tally takes a number of tumbles learning to ride the hoverboard, but master it she does, and this skill becomes central to all three novels. Her first heart-pounding plummet through the rollercoaster gap makes "her vision strangely clear," and subsequently, Tally begins to see past the rhetoric she has been fed to truly wonder about the Rusties. Her mind and eyes open, allowing her to consider that she and Shay may indeed have a choice about their faces and their futures. Interestingly, once Tally is on her solo journey to the Smoke, she experiences many falling nightmares, no doubt due to the unknown perils before her, symbolic of the fears she must face down in the dark unconscious before she can re-emerge to the light of knowing. Of course, the dark unconscious is the world of the Smoke, where she battles the elements and her own guilt, where she learns to work, to live in community, to love, and to pee outdoors. Here she also learns about the treachery of her city: that the operation "changes the way you think," creating "masses of smiling pretties, and a few people left to run things," in perfect control of a pretty-headed population. Eyes wide open and heart a-pitter-patter for less-than-perfect prince David, Tally determines not to return to the city, but inadvertently betrays all she loves when she tosses her tracking pendant into the fire. Part of Tally becoming a heroine is her recognizing her responsibility—intentional or not—for the raid and capture of her friends. With this realization comes another: no one should be forcibly altered. And she, Tally Youngblood, must

---

[2] To borrow from Jerome Kern and Dorothy Fields's song "Pick Yourself Up (Dust Yourself Off)."

attempt Maddy's cure in order to redeem herself and to save Shay and the others.

Arguably, falling in love with Zane in *Pretties* is one of Tally's biggest *falls*; it governs many of her actions in second and third books. Both helper figure and prince charmant, Zane is crucial to Tally's reawakening in New Pretty Town. But equally essential are her physical descents that serve to thrust bubbleheaded Tally-wa up to bubbly Tally Youngblood.

With her initial bungee jacket leap from Valentino Mansion comes a dawning reawakening: Specials plus Croy plus adrenaline rush equals clarity. (Of course, kissing also seems to help arouse her memory, too, it must be noted. Part of that whole *falling* in love thang.) As a result, Tally remembers David and the message from Croy. She climbs the transmission tower, nearly tumbling to her death, yet "her mind felt clean, like the air after a morning rain, and Tally understood at last why she had climbed up here. Not to impress Zane or the Smokies, or to pass any test, but because some part of her had wanted this moment, this clarity she hadn't felt since the operation." Once she finds the key to open the roof-top shed door, all hell breaks loose.[3] Zane and Tally each take one pill of a two-pill cure, and events spiral wildly from that moment. Clearly, Special Circumstances is watching, even wooing her, and she and the ailing Zane must leave New Pretty Town for the New Smoke, Shay and others in their company. Their ruse to rouse awareness, the Absolute Vodka Experiment that collapses the sky ice rink, not only sends a strong signal to the New Smokies, but also transforms Tally, who imagines herself delivering a speech to fellow Pretties about the operation, divulging "the terrible price of

---

[3] Think of other mythical and fairy tale heroines whose curiosity overtakes them: Eve, Pandora, Bluebeard's wife. Unlocking secrets always leads to trouble. T is for Tally is for Trouble.

being pretty—that lovely meant brainless, and that their easy lives were empty." This momentous fall "awaken[s] something larger" in our heroine, who consequently determines not to forget who she is, not to yield to the temptations of devilish Dr. Cable, not to let a little thing like a leap from a hot-air balloon stop her from escaping. This latter hurdle lands her alone and back in the wild, fully self-reliant, where she encounters the hunters and learns from Andrew that they were the guinea pigs for the operation, and are contained on a reservation and under the city's observation and domination.

Upon finally reaching the New Smoke, Tally deliberates over her responsibility for Zane's deterioration, upsetting David's life, and betraying Shay, and the fact that nothing is uncomplicated; no one is completely culpable or blameless. Her most significant moment of understanding comes after "a *plunge* into freezing water [*italics added*]": "Maybe she didn't need a handsome prince to stay awake—or an ugly one, for that matter. After all, Tally had cured herself without the pill and had made it all the way here on her own. . . . Maybe she'd always been bubbly, somewhere inside." With this self-knowledge firmly in her grip, Tally resolves to stay with Zane and not betray him and to somehow make the cure available for the whole city.

Precipitous falls precipitate further lessons for Tally in *Specials*. Her first is a half-slide/half-fall down the side of Pulcher Mansion to Zane's window. Though her Special senses render her unafraid of heights or falling, they do nothing to prepare her for the sight of an infirm and shaky Zane. From him she discovers that there are growing numbers of rebels in New Pretty Town. More importantly, Zane challenges Tally to rewire herself again as she did before: "'Undo what they did to you. . . . You can change yourself, Tally.'" With his urging, so begins Tally's re-evaluation of all things Special. Despite her super-human abilities and continual assurances that she is an

Übermensch,[4] our young heroine realizes that the one constant in her ugly, pretty, and special lives has been love. Seeing Zane so average has shaken and repulsed her; he is distant and she, untouchable. Suddenly, Tally measures the price for being special: "'I don't want to *see* this way! I don't want to be disgusted by everyone who's not part of our clique.'" Nothing like a little fall to shake the heroine from her arrogance and conformity.

Her next descent out in the wild is a doozie. A mixture of disgust and self-disgust after kissing her beloved propels her over the "chalky cliff" and into the "churning ocean." Lesser heroines would have succumbed to the undercurrent, but Tally breaks the water's surface—in another of her several symbolic rebirth moments—and eventually returns to shore. Physically up to any challenge, she nonetheless recognizes "how weak she really [is]," but that the wild is changing her and the alternative to her unwanted Special-ness lies within herself. When she hurls herself over a second cliff, the Overlook in Diego, her severe injuries render her unable to resist being apprehended. Thus begin the last lessons of Tally Youngblood, and they are dire, indeed.

Considered a "dangerous weapon" by her captors, Tally is scheduled to be operated on yet again and against her will. She is informed that her Special mind was previously altered so to be easily incited to "'anger or euphoria, countersocial impulses or feelings of superiority.'" Adamant that she will not be cut again—either by her own or a surgeon's hand—Tally battles her way free, with assistance from a now not-so-special Shay. While she learns that Shay no longer hates her, Tally also accepts her own separateness, that distance between herself and others that has persisted throughout all three books, despite her best efforts otherwise. However, she is convinced

---

[4] Or a *superman* (woman) in the sense philosopher Friedrich Nietzsche intended. His character Zarathustra in *Thus Spoke Zarathustra* shares the repulsion Tally feels when he asserts that ordinary man compared to Superman is "a laughingstock or a painful embarrassment."

of her responsibility to defend Diego and the New System from Dr. Cable's aggression. In the aftermath of the attack, a sober Tally reflects that given what Special Circumstances had wrought, "being *average* didn't seem pathetic. . . . Seeing what her own city had done had somehow made her feel less special." She commits to returning to New Pretty Town to confess her part with Shay in storming the Armory, the trigger for the retaliation upon Diego.

## The Heroine, Alone

An essential thing to note amidst all Tally's initiating and testing, questing and adventuring, is that she is often alone.

Being a heroine can really bite.

But that's the way it's done in the tales of legend and myth and folk and lore. Solo. Much to our young heroine's loneliness and chagrin. At the beginning of *Uglies*, lonesome Tally longs to be reunited with her BFF Peris. At its conclusion, she steps willingly into the jaws of the dragon with the notably singular assertion of her selfhood, "I'm Tally Youngblood. Make me pretty." When we rejoin her in *Pretties*, Tally wants nothing more than to *belong* to the Crims, yet senses the tenuousness of her new life, a "weird missingness" that leaves her feeling outside and different, and that "everything suck[s]." By the end of the second novel, though Tally has determined not to be parted from Zane, that is exactly what happens as she undergoes yet another body/mind-altering operation, this time against her will. In the opening chapter of *Specials*, although she is part of the Cutters' interlocking network, she admits to still feeling "outside and icy and *better*" than the ordinaries who make up New Pretty Town, and she becomes distressed and alarmed at her repulsion to Zane, who, because of his infirmity, is lost to her unless he too undergoes the operation to become Special. Of course, near the conclusion of the third novel Zane is dead, and Tally, utterly alone, is left again to consider a solitary future.

Which brings us to the central question of this essay: Why does the prince have to bite it?

## Why the Prince Bites It

Zane. He of the luscious lips and ink-black hair and metallic-gold eyes. The boy who boosted her to bubbly with merely a kiss. "The ultimate reason that Tally Youngblood wasn't merely just another bubblehead, happy and clueless among the spires of New Pretty Town" because Shay had first learned the secret route to the Smoke from him back in the ugly days (*Specials*). Zane, Tally's handsome prince. Why does he have to die?

Once upon a time there was a princess locked in a high tower with pretty clothes in closets and mirrors along the walls that told her daily how special she was. Like her literary cousin, the famous Lady of Shallot, eventually the princess grew tired of looking in mirrors that cast unattractive shadows of who she really was. Instead, she gazed longingly out the window toward the wild world. But there was no way out of the inaccessible tower, also guarded by an evil dragon cleverly disguised as a brilliant doctor.

Early on a young prince had tried to rescue her. He was not particularly comely, but he had a good heart and saw the best in hers. Sadly, the prince had little luck finding a ladder.

Later, a second prince managed to reach her, and though he was beautiful and a pretty fine kisser, he was crippled in the rescue attempt.

Heartbroken, the princess sought to help her injured beloved. There was nothing for the desperate girl to do except to jump from the tower. So she did. And her solitary fall "changed the story completely" (*Specials*).

This is, after all, Tally's quest, not Zane's. Tally's survival and self-actualization require that she not demur to the dudes or rely on passive subordination. Thus, she herself must ride the hoverboard, return posthaste to New Pretty Town, defeat the dragon (or de-activate Dr. Cable's Specialness), rise from the goo of re-birth (the viscous liquid of the operating tank), and save the day. In order to be a true heroine, Tally must liberate Tally before she can liberate or save the world. She learns that freedom, like knowledge, is a double-edged sword; that freedom, while preferable to empty-headed, pointless meandering from party to party and to blind and rigid obedience, can cut like a knife and has a "way of destroying things" (*Specials*). The princess is freed from the tower by her own volition: "no one would change her against her will, not ever again. There would be no more Special Circumstances" (*Specials*) because with full self-possession, Tally will never forget who she is, will keep herself special, and does not "need Special Circumstances to feel alive" (*Pretties*).

In a final exercise of heroic will, Tally determines to keep intact her special body, instincts, and skills, and to go forth and save the world. Her wolfishness denotes the outlaw who will continue to rail against the "gods," and as mythographer Marina Warner reflects,[5] "the beastly or less than human becomes an index of alienation, and often of one's own otherness; the story relates the possibility of acceptance, an end to the ache of longing to belong." Though Shay, Dr. Cable, and David reassure Tally that she is not alone, ambiguity about her future still persists at the conclusion of *Specials*. Tally Youngblood is the last of her kind.

But "maybe she doesn't have to [save the world] alone" (*Specials*). Though David didn't do "a very good job of saving [her]" (thank goodness and Scott Westerfeld), Tally knows he will always "remember who she really [is]" (*Specials*). Not bad for a helpmeet; David is to Adam as Tally is to Eve, except that she's the boss in their brave new world.

---

[5] In *From the Beast to the Blonde*.

Being solitary, isolated from people—Tally's biggest fear at the beginning of the series—is essential to her becoming Tally. In that process (granted, with some help from friends and frenemies), lies her full awakening: sexual, intellectual, moral, and emotional. No self-respecting heroine would hand the reins over to the prince or let him wield the sword. In this series, in order for Tally to wear the proud mantle of heroine, the prince must die. Scott Westerfeld does not wimp out on Tally, and she does not wimp out on the reader.

Will she live HEA? Who's to say? Would Tally Youngblood want such a life anyway? After all, the fully self-actualized Tally Young-blood has only just begun. As philosopher Ernst Bloch claimed, per-haps "*true genesis is not at the beginning, but at the end*, and it starts to begin only when society and existence become radical." Totally rad Tally, living on the edge, from the outside looking in on a rap-idly changing society, is just coming into her own. Only a bubble-head wishes for the eternally happy and empty and meaningless. Our heroine wants and deserves much more. Therein lies her true beauty. Maybe Angela Carter had Youngblood prophetically in mind when she uttered[6] the utopian goal of the fairy tale: "one day we might be happy, even if it won't last."

And isn't it pretty to think so?

---

Gail Sidonie Sobat is the author of six books, including the award-winning YA fantasy trilogy *Ingamald*, *A Winter's Tale*, and *A Glass Darkly*. Her most recent novel, *Gravity Journal*, a realistic novel about a young girl struggling with cutting and an eating disorder, is nomi-nated for a White Pine Award. Gail lives and writes in Canada, but has toured throughout her country, the U.S., and as far away as Doha, Qatar. She hopes someday to ride a hoverboard! Visit her website at www.gailsidoniesobat.com.

---

[6] In her introduction to *Old Wives' Fairy Tale Book*.

# A *Special* Hero

## J. FitzGerald McCurdy

In some ways, the Uglies trilogy is one long battle between Tally and Dr. Cable. Every turn in the story tests who has the stronger will, the evil enforcer or the indomitable rebel, the villain or the hero.

But in this essay, J. FitzGerald McCurdy notes a few disturbing similarities between Tally and Dr. Cable. Both of them know exactly what they want, after all, and will cause trouble for anyone who gets in their way. Both of them have a vision for the world. Both of them started as tricky uglies.

Are they really such opposites? Or simply two sides of the same coin?

IN FICTION, HEROES AND villains are usually main characters, often in opposition to one another. Heroes are distinguished by their exceptional courage, fortitude, and boldness, while villains are depicted as egregiously wicked, corrupt, or malevolent.

In the Uglies series, Dr. Cable is clearly the villain. Her lust for power and control is right up there with that of our world's most notorious bad guys, Josef Stalin and Adolf Hitler. And like those historic villains, Cable is a sociopath who will do whatever it takes, even murder, to maintain the status quo, convinced that the end—keeping the population in its cage to protect the world—justifies the means. When Special Circumstances attacks the Smoke at her instruction and kills the Boss, the cantankerous middle-aged ugly who looks after the Smoke's collection of old Rusty magazines, Cable displays neither regret for her troops' excessive use of violence nor remorse over the old man's death. After Tally and Shay accidentally destroy the Armory by letting nanos loose, Cable blames it on neighboring city Diego, which provides her with an excuse to attack them. Later, she confesses to Tally that she knew the truth all along, but lied so she could punish Diego for supporting the Smoke and taking in her city's runaways.

While even our history's worst villains possessed a sentimental streak—Hitler displayed an almost maudlin concern for injured or ill-treated animals, and Stalin choked with emotion whenever he gazed upon his favorite work of art—there is nothing sentimental about Cable. She was perhaps moved initially by the desire to prevent a dangerous return to Rusty times, but in her enforcement of the rules she herself created for Tally's city, she has come to despise the very people she is supposed to protect. When Tally questions the operation that changes people's brains in *Pretties*, Cable's answer reveals her true feelings about humankind: "Left alone, human beings are a plague. They multiply relentlessly, consuming every resource, destroying everything they touch. Without the operation, human beings always become Rusties."

For Cable, "humanity is a disease" and "Special Circumstances is the cure" (*Pretties*). After years of abusing the powers bestowed upon her by a rather benign Council, her increased use of violence is a natural progression. Her new *special* Specials—with their teeth filed to points; cold, black irises in dark, predatory, wolf-like eyes; "bones made from aircraft ceramics, light as bamboo and hard as diamonds"; and muscles constructed of "sheathed whips of self-repairing monofilament"—symbolize that violence (*Specials*). They are Cable's elite guard, created to fight, to hurt, to kill.

Sickened by Cable's attack on Diego, Tally asks, "When does it all end?" Cable replies:

> It never ends. I'm getting too much done that I could never do before, and believe me, the bubbleheads are having such fun watching it on the newsfeeds. And all it took was a *war*, Tally. I should have thought of this years ago . . . Don't you see, we've entered a new era. From now on, *every day* is a Special Circumstance! (*Specials*)

Cable's response is arrogant and chilling, especially the way she dismisses war as a simple means to an end. As Shay notes, Cable intends to take over Diego, remake it: "Turn it into another city just like ours: strict and controlled, *everyone* a bubblehead" (*Specials*). Fortunately, in attempting to extend her control over Diego, she goes too far and is finally stopped.

By our hero, Tally.

But are Tally and Dr. Cable really so different?

They share a few superficial similarities, of course, even beyond the ones that come with being raised in the same society. For one thing, they both possess a sarcastic edge: In *Uglies*, Cable says, "I suppose I should have been worried about you, out in the wild all alone. Poor Tally," and it doesn't require an especially vivid imagination to hear sarcasm dripping from each word of Tally's reply: "Thanks for your concern." They're both intelligent, and natural leaders, as well. And as Shay observes to Tally, "In a lot of ways, you and Dr. Cable are alike. You're both convinced you've personally got to change the world" (*Uglies*).

The important difference between them is the way they go about that goal. While Tally possesses many of Dr. Cable's attributes, she doesn't aspire to toppling governments (at least not initially), or wearing a crown, or controlling people. She's not power-hungry. Dr. Cable lives to enforce rules. Tally, on the other hand, lives to break them.

Tally is identified as a rule-breaker early in *Uglies*. When we meet her on the first page, she has already tricked the dorm minder and is about to cross the river into New Pretty Town, a forbidden activity. For Tally, breaking the rules—pushing the limits—is exciting. Equally exciting is the fear of getting caught. But this is infantile stuff—potty training for what is to come.

Usually breaking the rules—breaking the law—is a bad thing. But what if you live in a society where people are oppressed, like in India during the time of Gandhi, or where people are controlled through violence and terror like in Russia and Germany under Stalin and Hitler, or through brain surgery as in Tally's world? What if the leaders, the ones making the rules, are terrorists, assassins, kidnappers, or bank robbers—villains who crush the bodies and spirits of their own people and climb to absolute power over the bodies of millions of murdered citizens? What if the very society to which they belong is corrupt and evil? Wouldn't those conditions justify some serious rule-breaking in order to bring about change for the better?

Tally's leap from childish pranks to serious rule-breaking is triggered by her discovery that her city is not the ideal place she has always believed it to be—that the pretty-making surgery doesn't just change the way you look, but "the way you think." From that moment on, Tally's breaking of the rules is purpose-driven, and that rule-breaking results in vast, sweeping changes that affect not only her own city, but the entire world . . . for the better.

Tally's reasons for breaking the rules are important. In her world, Dr. Cable and Company control people's minds and bodies in order to prevent what happened to the Rusties from ever happening again. The entire pretty population is constantly spaced-out, drunk, and supposedly, happy. It seems to work, at first glance. There's no crime, no anger, no wars, no poverty, no deaths, no worries, no need for money, no pollution, no SUVs. But there's a darker side. Pretties resort to surgery to add ever more glam to their already Barbie doll–perfect features—a creepy form of self-mutilation that speaks volumes about the dangers of a totally hedonistic lifestyle—not to mention cut themselves and pop calorie purgers to feel . . . *something*. There are no fundamental exchanges of ideas, no exciting plans for the future, no greater purpose. The course of each person's life is fixed. Cable can claim that people have the option of choice as much as she wants, but she's a liar. There are no choices except no-brainers like what to have for lunch or what to wear or whether to drink champagne, again. The people of Tally's city may appear happy and bubbly, but they are even more oppressed than the people of India in Gandhi's time.

And this is where Cable and Tally butt heads. Tally wants to be herself, not someone else's creation. She wants the freedom to make her own choices about the things that affect her life. Further, she believes that everyone should have that fundamental right. But Cable keeps getting in her way, and Tally has no choice but to push back. She just happens to save the world in the process. Like fellow rule-breaker Gandhi, a man of conscience who broke the rules not by choice but by necessity, Tally significantly alters the course of history. It's what rule-breakers do.

Except, remember, Dr. Cable used to be a rule-breaker too. She's still a rule-breaker, in a way; she and her Specials enforce the rules by breaking them (though, unlike with Tally, breaking the rules for them has nothing to do with freedom of choice and everything to do with control). But like Tally, Cable was also tricky when she was an ugly: "I was just like you," Cable tells Tally in *Pretties*. "All of us [Specials] were. We went to the ruins, tried to run farther, had to be brought back. That's why we let uglies play their little tricks—to see who's cleverest. To see which of you fights your way out of the cage." Because that's how Cable finds her Specials in the first place.

This notion of rule-breakers becoming rule-enforcers, like the Specials and Dr. Cable herself, isn't exclusive to the Uglies series. We're all familiar with stories of computer hackers who end up working as security consultants for computer companies, helping those companies keep their networks secure from other potential hackers, and the stories of convicted felons who find employment in Vegas or other gambling meccas, enforcing rules in the very casinos they used to cheat. The BBC reported recently that as part of a drive aimed at addressing a shortfall of police officers in London, even Scotland Yard has relaxed its ban on recruiting ex-criminals to its ranks.

In these cases, the transformation from rule-breakers to rule-enforcers is considered a good thing—the former rule-breakers are now working *for* society instead of *against* it. But this transformation doesn't always turn out so well. After all, Stalin and Hitler started out as idealistic rule-breakers too.

Which means that despite all the good she's done, Tally herself has the potential to become as much of a villain as Dr. Cable.

Remember how Tally is in *Uglies*? All she wants is to be pretty. When Shay chooses to run away instead of having the pretty-making surgery, Tally thinks she's insane to want to stay ugly. But the Tally we see at the end of *Specials* is no longer that Tally. She's come a long way since then; she's brought about a new world order in which people are free to make their own choices. Now, she tells us, she has to protect the fragile planet from the very people she has freed.

Appointing herself and David as the official guardians of the world is a noble cause that carries with it an awesome responsibility, but also the inherent danger that, as the burgeoning cities push into the wild, she'll be forced to restrict others' choices, just as Cable did. In *Extras*, she seems to have acquired a hard edge and an arrogance that weren't evident in her before, even as a new Special. When she first appears halfway through the book, the first words out of her mouth are, "My name's Tally Youngblood. Sorry to disturb you, but this is a special circumstance." And when Aya mentions that since Tally saved everyone from the Prettytime, her city will give her any assistance she needs, Tally says, "I'm not interested in their help." Aya thinks Tally is refusing assistance because she's worried that Aya's city might have built the inhumans' weapon, but Tally just shrugs. "I wouldn't say worried. In fact, that would make things simpler. Governments have been brought down before, after all . . . By me."

Her reaction reminds me of Dr. Cable, and the words Shay shouts at Tally in anger in *Pretties*: "No cure is going to make you any different—you were busy betraying people a long time ago. You didn't need any operation to make you selfish and shallow and full of yourself. You already were."

Tally and Cable share a few more questionable qualities than being tricky and using a little sarcasm. They are also alike in their ability to tell lies and use others to achieve their own ends. When Cable tells Tally in *Uglies* that the little heart pendant finder will only respond to Tally's eye-print, she's lying. On Tally's part, she invents a very plausible story to explain her trip to the Smoke and allay the Smokies' suspicions that she's a spy—which, in fact, she is (at first). And, just as Cable blackmails Tally by displaying on the wallscreen an image of Tally as she looks at that moment—"puffy-eyed and disheveled, exhaustion and red scratches marking her face, her hair sticking out in all directions, and her expression turning horrified as she beheld her own appearance" (*Uglies*)—and telling her that she will look like that forever if she doesn't betray her friends and lead Special Circumstances to the Smoke, Tally shows that she too can use people, as she uses Aya as bait to draw out the inhumans in *Extras*.

At the end of *Specials*, Tally makes herself a rule-enforcer, and like Cable, in that role Tally is accountable to no one but herself. According to Aya, her voice in *Extras* is like razors—sound familiar? When Tally is brought before Cable for the first time and tries to act dumb about her relationship with Shay, she can't help but notice the edge in Cable's voice as it suddenly becomes as "sharp as a razor blade" (*Uglies*). (During that brief encounter, "razor-blade voice" is repeated twice, and Cable's voice is described the same way several more times over the next three books.)

Not only is Tally's voice razor-sharp like Cable's but her speech in *Extras* sounds more like Cable's than Tally's in the Uglies series. It's often both tough and threatening. When Frizz's Radical Honesty surge compels him to blurt out the truth about Tally to the inhumans, Tally wants to leave him behind in the crashing hovercar, calling him a moron and a freak. Tally acts rashly multiple times in *Extras*, neglecting to discuss problems with others before acting. Particularly disturbing is her display of poor judgment when she begins blowing up the inhumans' spaceships because she's convinced that they're weapons, and that Udzir and the inhumans are planning to destroy the world, when in fact they're trying to save it. Even Shay admits that when Tally gets a plan in her head, "it's easier just to go along. Otherwise, you'll find out that Tally can be very, very special."

Well, Tally *is* special. She's the last of Cable's *special* Specials. That's why Cable rescues her at the end of *Specials*. "You're the only real Cutter left," says Cable. "The last of my Specials designed to live in the wild, to exist outside the cities. . . . I don't want my work to become extinct."

In carrying out Cable's work, is Tally turning into another Dr. Cable? We'll have to wait and see. In the meantime, David, Shay, and her other friends would be well advised to keep their eyes on her.

---

J. FitzGerald McCurdy is the author of the bestselling fantasy trilogy The Serpent's Egg. Her latest series, The Mole Wars, follows the adventures of Steele and his companions in the world of the Mole People in the tunnels and passageways under New York City. A retired lawyer, McCurdy also worked as a documentary film writer. She lives in Ottawa, Canada, and is working on her seventh book. Visit her Web site at www.jfitzgeraldmccurdy.com.

# Challenging the Gods

## Rosemary Clement-Moore

Way before she was a Smokey, a revolutionary, or a Special, Tally was one very important thing—she was tricky. Her need to fool minders and crash parties and break rules is the spark of the story. Quite simply, without Tally's tricks the rest of her adventures would never have gotten started.

Of course, Tally is not the first tricky character to inhabit the pages of a book, or the pages of history, for that matter. Here, Rosemary Clement-Moore takes us on a tour of notable tricksters both real and legendary, and compares their rule-breaking and society-remaking stunts to those in the Uglies series.

In this essay, you'll find Tally in some unexpected company, from Greek gods to Russian composers to Time Lords. A motley crew to be sure, but they all know one thing: that a good prank—like a good kiss—can change the world.

I SHOULD HAVE KNOWN the Prettiverse wouldn't be pretty.

Any book that starts out by comparing the sky to cat vomit is probably not going to be full of unicorns and rainbows. Not unless the unicorns are surgically engineered special police and the rainbows are really the artificial light reflecting off the metaphorical fog of your nanotech-induced complacency.

Strange as it seems, I mean it as a compliment when I say that the Uglies series scared and depressed me. This type of book, which eggheads and English teachers call "dystopian fiction," makes you think about what's wrong with the world. It's built on things that are messed up in our society right now, and shows very clearly where we could be headed if things don't change. That can be a real downer.

Fortunately, the Prettiverse has two things: hoverboards (which are, let's face it, just plain cool), and Tally Youngblood, who uses her hoverboard to elevate pranking to an art form. So at the same time I was lamenting over how easily our present world could become her apocalyptic past, I was eagerly turning pages, anxious to see what would happen next.

Even before she knows she's going to bring the mind-rain that changes the Prettiverse forever, Tally is a rebel. So are Shay, David, Maddie, and all the Cutters and the Smokies. So was Zane. Tally, though, is the trickiest and most rebellious of them all, her lawless brain continually resetting the boundaries imposed on her by both society and science. And if we look at our own history, we can see other bubbly thinkers who have transformed our culture. People who, like Tally, do the unexpected, break the rules, and change the world.

## Tricksters and Rebel Gods

Human beings are strange creatures. We don't just *like* conformity, we're engineered for it. As a species and a society, we tend to ostracize those who are too different. From an evolutionary perspective, this makes sense, but sociologically it can lead to the equivalent of inbreeding: cultural stagnation and complacency.

Maybe that's why people around the world have legends of disobedient characters who bring needed change to the world. There are gods like Loki in Scandinavia, the Monkey-King in China, and Coyote in the traditions of the Native American Southwest. Other tales feature animals, like Anansi the spider, in Eastern African stories, and Br'er Rabbit, a combination of Native and African-American folktales.

These trickster characters are always wily and clever (even though their vanity or pride can make them rash or foolish), and their actions are often not very heroic in the traditional sense. They hoax and manipulate, they break rules, and they always shake up the status quo. The trickster is a character who makes things happen and challenges the system.

From the moment we meet Tally, she's breaking the rules. She ditches her interface ring and sneaks via an old bridge—one that can't talk—into New Pretty Town to crash a party, where no uglies are allowed. When she's discovered, she's clever enough to set off the fire alarm for a distraction, and then bungees from the roof to escape, certainly a daring, boundary-breaking move.

Zane is inspired by Tally's rule-breaking behavior to create what is essentially a clique of tricksters: the Crims. But it's Tally—as Shay points out later in *Extras*—who makes things happen. She's not an instrument of small change, but of big, world-altering transformation.

Tally is a lot like Prometheus this way. Prometheus was a Greek god, like Zeus and his buddies on Mount Olympus. However, he felt like the gods didn't have enough compassion for the mortals on earth, whom Zeus and the others viewed as ignorant primitives. Prometheus liked the scrappy human upstarts, and so he stole the gods' knowledge of fire and gave it to the mortals so they didn't have to live in the dark.

Zeus was pissed. He ordered Prometheus to be chained to a mountain, where every day an eagle would come and eat his liver. Since Prometheus was immortal, he never actually died; every night his liver grew back and every day the eagle came and ate it all over again. If that's not a caution against disobeying the gods, I don't know what is.

Prometheus's gift was more than just a literal light-the-night, cook-your-food type of fire. This was divine fire—the ability to think and create and reason, which had up until then been the sole province of the gods—and it sparked the rise of humankind. Mere mortals began developing culture, art, and literacy. They were no longer imprisoned in the dark of ignorance.

Compare the savageness of the pre-Rusty reservation in *Pretties* to the pre-fire description of humans in the Prometheus myth. The violent primitives are being kept in the dark by the god-like scientists from Tally's city. Tally, like Prometheus, is one of the gods, and the "fire" that she brings to the reservation is the idea that just because something has always been one way doesn't mean that it always has to stay like that.

Not everyone jumps on board with this. In fact, Andrew Simpson Smith is pretty much alone in his tentative acceptance of the concept of thinking for oneself. But by the time he encounters Tally again in *Specials*, he has become a trickster himself, crossing the boundaries of the reservation and breaking the rules by helping runaways escape to Diego.

Tally's role, in some ways, might also be compared to the serpent's in the Garden of Eden. Unlike Prometheus (and Tally), the serpent is a trickster character without any altruistic motivation. He's just jealous and stirring up trouble. True to his archetype, the serpent uses Adam and Eve's own disobedient natures against them.

Let's face it. Humans aren't that hard to talk into disobeying the rules (e.g., "Don't eat from that one tree over there"). Humans eat from the tree and gain knowledge and reason, but they are evicted from paradise, and the serpent is punished by having to crawl on his belly forever, the lowest of the low.

New Pretty Town certainly seems like paradise. Most people don't even realize they're trading a big chunk of their brain in return for their idyllic life. (And a lot of them—the ones who probably don't miss that part anyway—would think it was a fair bargain.)

In engineering the big prank at the floating ice rink, Tally and Zane encourage the disobedient nature of the Crims to accomplish their own goal. Their compatriots see this as a big bubbly lark, but few of them really know what bubbly means, other than a temporary adrenaline high.

Tally isn't acting maliciously or frivolously, but her actions have far-reaching consequences. The collapse of the ice rink, as Tally and Zane intend, sends a message to the New Smoke, furthering their plans to escape. The chain of events that comes from Tally trying to fix her own brain leads (a book, a war, and a lot of surge later) to free thinking for everyone, but also figurative eviction from paradise.

I like to think of Tally as a Prometheus more than a serpent, but you can't ignore that the gift of fire she brought to her world is a mixed blessing.

Tricksters bring change, and just as change can have a good side and a bad side, so can the characters that trigger it. The object of Br'er Rabbit's shenanigans is usually a deserving target, but you have to admit, he's not a guy you'd trust alone with your stuff. Still, while the trickster does break rules, she usually takes aim not at the laws that keep us safe, but the arbitrary rules that hold us back and hold us down.

Sometimes, however, there's a more defined split in the nature of the trickster. As much as I'd like to stay all literary, the best example of the two sides of the trickster is a modern one. I'm talking, of course, about Doctor Who and his arch-nemesis, the Master, from the old and new versions of the British television series.

Doctor Who is a Time Lord—a human-looking alien who can travel through time and space in a craft that looks (stay with me here) like a big blue phone booth. Doctor Who has elements of the crafty and clever trickster in him, and he's part Prometheus as well—an alien with almost god-like abilities when compared to mere mortals, whom he rescues again and again from other-worldly dangers. Though he's made some vengeful decisions in the past, the Doctor is generally more about the preservation of life than the destruction of it.

Contrast that with his arch-nemesis, the Master. From the same alien race as the Doctor, the Master is all the same things—wily trickster and god-like alien—but he's all about destruction and/or world domination.

Which brings me to Dr. Cable. In *Pretties*, when Dr. Cable first suggests that Tally join the Specials, Tally asks her what she was like as an ugly. "Outstanding," says Dr. Cable, and Tally realizes the doctor was tricky, like her.

Dr. Cable has all the earmarks of a trickster. She has no trouble breaking rules—actually, she doesn't even think rules exist for her. She has god-like powers of surgical transformation. She certainly likes to scheme. Like the serpent in the garden, she manipulates Tally, using her desire for the pretty surgery to get her to follow Shay into the Smoke. She plays on Tally's emotions, and she's good at predicting what Tally will do next, perhaps because they're so much alike.

But how are they different, other than the fact that Dr. Cable does bad things and Tally tries to counter them? To answer that, we need a little historical perspective.

## Out of Bounds Isn't Always a Bad Thing

History may be written by the victor, according to a Latin proverb (and the Romans would know), but history is *made* by the rule-breakers. And by rule-breaker, I don't necessarily mean law-breaker. Sometimes they're the same thing, but not always. What I mean is someone who thinks outside of what is normal for her situation.

"Normal" is a relative thing. What's normal for Tally is not normal for us. I'm not talking about hoverboards and surge and the perpetual party of New Pretty Town, but Tally's entire frame of reference for acceptable looks, thoughts, and actions. For example, those ancient magazines that the Boss preserved in the Smoke were probably tabloids like *People* and *Us*—full of celebrities who are beautiful to us, but "ugly" to Tally's eyes.

Most attributes of a group—height, weight, health, smarts, artistic talent, etc.—have what statisticians call a "normal distribution" or "bell curve." If you measure the height of everyone in your class and plot it on a graph, you'd have a big hump in the middle, where most people are "average height," and it would fall off on the sides, where you have some people who are shorter or taller, and then eventually maybe just one or two who are *really* short or *really* tall.

This is relatively simple when dealing with numbers, like height, weight, or grade point average. It gets more complicated when you're dealing with subjective experiences, like beauty and behavior.

There's a theory in politics called the Overton Window that describes how there's a range, or window, of what the public views as acceptable policy, and how that view of what's acceptable is changed. Remember how $2.50 for a gallon of gas used to seem outrageously expensive? Then the price went up to $3.50 a gallon, and we started praying for it just to go down to under $3. All of a sudden, $2.50 started to sound cheap.

The Overton Window suggests that, if you want to institute a policy that's outside of what the public considers tolerable, you should propose something way more extreme than what you really want to happen. Say someone wants to ban cell phones from restaurants. First, they should propose that cell phones be unlawful in any public area. Then, after the public goes nuts in protest, they should say, "Okay, what if we *only* ban it from restaurants?" Public opinion on this new idea will be more accepting, because the initial proposal moved the window toward the right. Or left. I'm not sure if stringent cell-phone usage rules are liberal or conservative.

Tally experiences this phenomenon across all the books. Her eye gets used to what is normal in the Smoke, and she considers David attractive. But then once she gets used to the "normal" of New Pretty Town, he seems repulsive to her. Zane, on the other hand, seems beautiful, but when Tally becomes a Special, Zane's minor defects—things that even a Pretty might not notice—become disfiguring in her mind.

Like beauty, the normal range of behavior can be equally subjective. However, most people in any society fall within that big bump of "average" on the graph. Those free thinkers that lie on the outsides of the bell curve are the ones who make interesting things happen, for good or ill. Because while the bulk of people in a society go with the flow, on the fringes are those who shake things up. These are the outliers, the rule-breakers. They push themselves to be different, and through their actions, push the world to be different.

Picture a concert hall, where a huge crowd has gathered for the premiere of a new multi-media piece, live action combined with lights and sound. The curtain goes up, the musicians strike their discordant first notes, and the dancers begin their wild gyrations. The audience goes nuts, and not in a good way. They hate it and start a riot in the hall. They throw things at the stage, get into fights and brawls. The police have to rush in to restore peace.

Are you thinking rock concert in the eighties? The Who? Some head banging metal band? Think again.

This was Paris in 1913. The musical piece was Igor Stravinsky's *Rite of Spring*, accompanied by a ballet choreographed by Vaslav Nijinsky. (And I'll bet you thought classical music was boring.)

Stravinsky set out to knock the stuffy musical world on its ear, and he succeeded. No one had ever used the instruments in the orchestra like he did, and the rhythmic structure of the music was completely unknown. It went against the cadence that his audiences' brains considered normal, acceptable music.

We humans get used to a relative normal. When something comes along that is outside of "average" on that bell curve, we don't like it. In fact, we hate it . . . at least at first. Forty years after *Rite of Spring* caused a riot in Paris, it was included in Disney's *Fantasia*. And you don't get much more mainstream than Disney. Stravinsky is considered one of the most influential composers of the twentieth century because after that, musicians started writing music that shook people out of the expected rhythmic rut.

For Tally, thinking differently is almost like her superpower. Of all the tricky characters in the books—the runaways, the Smokies, the Crims, the Cutters—she is the only one who *thinks* her way out of whatever mental box she's been placed in, first by her society's complacency and the expectation of becoming a pretty and later by surgical alteration of her brain.

Other characters are able to achieve a clear-headed, "bubbly" state temporarily, through some scarily self-destructive means—going hungry, risking their lives, cutting themselves. But only Tally makes that permanent change, rewires her brain without the help of pain or pills.

It's by studying the way Tally's brain worked around the lesions that Maddie is able to manufacture a better, safer cure for the bubble-headed pretties. Tally's gift to the world is literally a new way of thinking!

Back to our past, and the nineteenth century, when painting was rigidly governed by the Academie des Beaux-Arts in Paris. When painters like Monet, Renoir, and Manet started to paint shocking pictures with unapproved subject matter and unconventional techniques, they were banned from the academy. Now we see Impressionist paintings as sedate and conventional compared to works of the innovators who came in the twentieth century, the cubists and surrealists and minimalists.

Like Jackson Pollock. A 1959 headline said about his painting, "This is not art—it's a joke in bad taste." Then in 2006, one of those jokes in bad taste became the world's most expensive painting when it sold for $140 million. Clearly that Overton Window of acceptability shifted, and the joke is now on those critics.

Why is this important? It's just music and painting, not life and death. But Jean-Jacques Rousseau, back in the eighteenth century, said, "The world of reality has its limits; the world of imagination is boundless." If you put limits on creativity in the arts, then you put limits on what human beings can imagine for the real world around us—which means you're putting limits on what human beings can do and be. (The writings of Rousseau inspired the leaders of the French Revolution. Definitely a man whose ideas shook the status quo.)

Throughout the books, we see Tally resetting the bar for bubbly behavior and experiences. She keeps doing things no one has done before, like jumping off a building in a bungee jacket in *Uglies* and climbing the transmission tower on top of Valentino Mansion in *Pretties*. Following her lead, the Crims go from a clique of fake criminals, going to parties in towers like everyone else and wearing the costumes of rule-breakers, to genuine tricksters, copying Tally and Zane, partying in the woods, and outwitting the wardens.

Like Stravinsky, Tally breaks the Crims out of the rut of predictable thinking. They begin to think differently, not just in a musical, rhythmic sense, but physiologically, as the adrenaline from rule-breaking pushes away the empty-headedness of being pretty. We see this new level of trickiness continuing in *Specials*, when Tally and Shay are having to, as part of Special Circumstances, guard against the same kind of parties and behavior they initiated as Crims. In *Extras*, this boundary-pushing trend continues with the Sly Girls and with those who do extreme things to raise their face rank.

But rule-breaking just for the sake of rule-breaking isn't enough. There's a difference between stepping outside the lines for shock value, and challenging the gods who want to keep you inside a box. Some rules, after all, are meant to keep us safe and help us coexist as a (relatively) civilized society. But some rules—usually the unwritten ones—are like the little totems hanging around the pre-Rusty reservation: designed to keep Andrew Simpson Smith's people inside their boundaries and prevent them from discovering how big the world really is.

The biggest changes occur when individuals, like Prometheus and the rebel tricksters of myth, challenge these figurative, totem gods of society. Galileo said the Earth went around the sun and not the other way around. Radical idea, right? Back then, you could be imprisoned for saying something that went counter to what the establishment held to be true—in this case, that the Earth was the center of the universe and everything else rotated around it.

How important is it to challenge complacent thinking? If Galileo had bowed to pressure, we'd still be in the Dark Ages, believing the world is flat and that diseases are caused by a build-up of evil spirits in the body. Instead, by continuing his experiments, Galileo became the father of modern physics, establishing the principles that kicked off the scientific revolution and brought Europe out of the Dark Ages and into the Renaissance.

It was Galileo who refined the compass, which allowed Magellan to sail all the way around the world and prove the Earth is not flat, which led to Christopher Columbus climbing on a boat and heading to the New World. Compare Galileo's effect on exploration with what Tally teaches Andrew Simpson Smith. He explains it to Aya at the end of *Extras*, as the inhumans are getting ready to launch themselves into the New World of space: The world has no edge, no end. You must learn to see beyond the little men.

Martin Luther was a sixteenth-century German religious scholar who had some questions about the way the Roman Catholic Church—at that time the only Church there was—did things. Talk about challenging the system. No one had ever questioned the Papal authority on anything. Martin Luther proposed that everyone should be able to read the Bible for themselves and shouldn't have to go through an ordained priest to talk to God.

Luther brought figurative and literal fire when his writings started the Protestant Reformation, a bloody war over religion that resonated through European politics and prejudices for centuries. But on the other hand, it led (eventually) in many places to freedom of religion, which gave individuals the right to choose what they want to believe or not believe.

Additionally, Martin Luther's challenge to the status quo meant the wildfire spread of literacy, since once the Bible was translated from Latin into languages that the common people spoke, they wanted to learn to read it for themselves. And reading caught on. Now people can read anything they want, and form their own opinions on it. For good or ill—or for both—Luther and the Reformation changed the course of Western civilization.

The freedom to think for oneself is exactly what Tally Youngblood brought to the pretties. This is the metaphorical fire from the gods that Prometheus gave to humankind. And here is the big difference between Tally and Dr. Cable. Tricksters do in myth and story what these outside-edges-of-the-bell-curve people have done throughout history. They make things happen. They make *change* happen.

Dr. Cable is about making change not happen. She uses her superpowers of surgical transformation to make the world into an obedient stagnant one she can control. Though she's a trickster, she's the opposite of Prometheus. Instead of enlightenment, she brings ignorance.

Tally Youngblood, on the other hand, brings illumination. When the mind-rain spread across all the cities in the world, people shook off their complacency and started questioning. But as Tally says at the end of *Specials*, freedom has a way of destroying things.

## Progress Is a Mixed Blessing

There's a significant sequel to the Prometheus legend that shows how giving fire to a society can have far reacting effects. To get back at the humans, the gods put all kinds of bad things in a box—war, pestilence, suspicion, hatred, despair, and disease—and gave it to girl named Pandora, to whom they also gave curiosity, so she couldn't help but open the box. When she did, all the good things that came from Prometheus' gift were balanced out.

I already mentioned Adam and Eve, and the parallels are pretty obvious. The first humans had an ideal situation in paradise. They just had to take care of the garden and not eat from the Tree of Knowledge. Well, of course they did (and of course this got blamed on the woman, but that's a subject for a different discourse), and it gave them the ability to reason. Finer theological points aside, like Prometheus's gift of fire this was the starting point for all human invention and endeavor. But it was also the beginning of jealousy, murder, war, disease. . . . This list should sound familiar.

Free will is a dangerous gift, just like divine fire. It opens the door to genius and invention, but it can also veer off into destructive extremes of hatred and violence. Once you give people the freedom to think for themselves, you also give them the freedom to make bad decisions.

Tally realizes this at the end of *Specials*, when she sends her manifesto to the world, warning that the new Special Circumstances will be watching, and waiting, in case the cities expand too far into the wilderness, threatening to repeat the Rusties' world destroying mistakes.

In *Extras*, three years after the mind-rain, and the end of the Prettytime, things have gone a little nuts. On one hand, people are certainly thinking for themselves (as much as humans ever do). But we also see a balance between conformity and boundary-pushing, as humans in Aya's city do radical things to their bodies but still operate as cliques.

Cities are growing, and so is technology that demands steel. Again, it's Andrew who encapsulates this point: More people, more cities, less wild. But the ball of the world doesn't get bigger. When steel supplies from the old Rusty cities start to run out, there's even talk of strip mining. Tally's new Special Circumstances has its work cut out for it, keeping watch.

There's also a new danger—or there seems to be, when Aya finds the mass driver tunnels that appear to be a weapon designed to destroy cities. The mere *possibility* of the invention of such weapons is a result of the freedom brought by the mind-rain. Pretties were too bubbleheaded to make war.

But this seeming danger is more of a solution than a threat, a new frontier, and once again, it's the result of extreme thinking. One of the best images for the two-sided coin of progress is voiced at the end of *Extras*. The same missiles designed to kill cities, carried human beings into space—"[d]eath and hope in one package."

The Prometheus story has one more tag at the end of it. After Pandora opened the box full of bad stuff—war and hatred and famine and disease—there was one thing left in the bottom of it. Hope. Cheesy, maybe, but that's how the story goes.

Dr. Cable might have been a misguided megalomaniac, who became a god to be rebelled against rather than an instrument of positive progress. But her last act was worthy of a true trickster—she released Tally to guard humans against our worst impulses, like hope from the bottom of Pandora's box.

I have to admit that I don't completely disagree with Dr. Cable's thinking that humans will destroy their world if left unchecked. Our complacency, our notion that this planet owes us everything it has, can lead us down the Rusty path to destruction. I can see how easy it would be to live an easy, perfectly pretty life and never ask questions.

Fortunately, I know we are an ornery, contrary species who doesn't like to be told what we can and cannot do. We don't need tricksters or gods or wizards or Time Lords to come and save us. Because before she was pretty or special, Tally Youngblood was human. And if the series says anything, then, it's that we humans have it within ourselves to *think* our way out of disaster.

Freedom has a way of destroying things. But it also gives us the ability to create, innovate, and change the course of our world for the better.

<hr />

Rosemary Clement-Moore is the author of smart, funny supernatural mystery novels. Her Maggie Quinn: Girl vs. Evil series (*Prom Dates From Hell*, *Hell Week*, *Highway to Hell*) features a psychic girl detective with a different way of looking at the world, and a best friend who is definitely on the outside of the bell curve. Rosemary's favorite tricksters are Puck from *A Midsummer Night's Dream*, Doctor Who (especially the ninth one), and of course, Bugs Bunny. But like everything in her life, this is subject to change without notice. You can find out the latest at her Web site, www.rosemaryclementmoore.com.

# Beauty Smackdown

## Our Society Versus New Pretty Town

### Janette Rallison

Books are important for the questions they make you ask—about your life, your values, and your world. That's one of the ways that stories, like a hoverboard ride or a kiss, can rewire your brain.

In this essay, Janette Rallison explores the questions she asked herself while reading the Uglies series. Some of these I definitely intended readers to ask themselves, but others are quite surprising. I suggest you read what follows with paper handy, ready to jot down your own answers. But make sure not to use a pen, because you may find them changing as you go.

I BELONG TO A book club. We generally spend fifteen minutes talking about the month's book and the rest of the two hours talking about our kids and husbands. (Plus we consume large amounts of chocolate. This is why I go.) When we read *Uglies*, we spent the entire time talking not only about the book, but about the series as well. Like many of the women in the book club, I couldn't stop at just one book. I had to find out what happened to Tally, David, Shay, and Zane. I also had to see who ended up pretty and whether or not it made them happy.

Science fiction authors are known for taking aspects of our society and magnifying them in their books, giving readers a chance to see what would happen if our present attitudes and practices were taken to the extreme. And as the titles suggest, one of the biggest issues in the series is how we view physical beauty. So what is Scott Westerfeld saying about beauty, and more importantly, is he correct?

In *Uglies* just about everybody wants to be good looking because attractive people have more benefits. And I'll admit right off that for the first few chapters of *Uglies,* I thought New Pretty Town was a great idea.

I don't mean the endless partying, the being drunk half the time, or the obsession with fashion. I just admired the fairness of it all.

New Pretty Town came to be because in the past, "everyone judged everyone else based on their appearance. People who were taller got better jobs, and people even voted for some politicians just because they weren't quite as ugly as everybody else. . . . People killed one another over stuff like having different skin color" (*Uglies*).

Tally has been taught that how we react to attractive people is built into us by "a million years of evolution. The big eyes and lips said: I'm young and vulnerable, I can't hurt you, and you want to protect me. And the rest said: I'm healthy, I won't make you sick. And no matter how you felt about a pretty, there was a part of you that thought: *If we had kids, they'd be healthy too. I want this pretty person*. . . . It was biology . . . like your heart beating, you couldn't help believing all these things, not when you saw a . . . pretty face" (*Uglies*).

But that's fiction. How important is being beautiful in our society?

When I was a teenager I read a book of difficult questions. One of them was: Would you choose to be beautiful if it meant you'd lose five years from your life span?

Would you?

Don't just skim the question; really answer it. How important is beauty to you? Important enough that you'd give away five years of your life for it?

The question bothered me because I knew the answer should be easy. Who in their right mind would trade part of their life—1,825 days—just to look good? Looking good doesn't have anything to do with the quality of your life.

But I kept finding myself wanting to refine the question. Exactly how ugly would I have to be to have that extra five years? And were we talking about a life span of seventy years? Eighty years? Only forty? The question just wouldn't go away. It hovered, revealing all sorts of uncomfortable things about myself and society—because let's face it, we do judge people based on looks.

Oh, as a society we like to pretend that we aren't really all that vain, that we don't obsess about our appearances, and that we're capable of seeing past all the superficial stuff. As Martin Luther King Jr. would say—if, you know, he happened to live in a Scott Westerfeld novel—"People should not be judged by the prettiness of their skin, but by the content of their character."[1]

---

[1] My apologies to Martin Luther King, Jr., for butchering his quote.

We throw around phrases to emphasize the point: Beauty is only skin deep. Beauty is as beauty does. It's what inside that really matters. You can't judge a book by its cover.[2]

Any high school freshman will tell you differently. As will your local plastic surgeon, or the person in charge of hiring models for advertisements.

If you want to sell something, you show a beautiful person holding, eating, wearing, or driving it. There is a reason we call beautiful people attractive. We are attracted to them just because of their looks. As a society we want to be them so badly that we will buy the soda we see them drinking, the clothes we see them wearing, and the cars we see them driving.

We can claim we aren't affected by looks, but the way we spend our money says differently. So have several clinical studies too boring to quote. In summary they basically say that good-looking people get more attention, more dates, better jobs, and even increased leniency in criminal sentences. I would put footnotes in here, but really, does anyone out there doubt this information?

So is it any wonder that I find New Pretty Town and all of its equality of looks a good idea?

Scott Westerfeld couldn't leave New Pretty Town a utopia though—perhaps because he wanted to mirror the other views our society has on appearances. As much as we idolize beauty, we often see beautiful people as shallow and stupid.

The stereotypes abound: the ding-y cheerleader, the vacuous Valley girl. We tell dumb blonde jokes. We insult guys by calling them pretty boys. If you're a movie director and you want to make a girl look smart, just give her glasses, bad hair, and unfashionable clothes because, hey, intelligent people couldn't possibly also be gorgeous.

---

[2] Every author knows that people do judge books by their covers, which is why we will openly weep whenever a marketing department slaps some hideous illustration on our novel.

When beauty pageant contestant Miss Teen South Carolina gave an incomprehensible answer on live TV filled with phrases like, "I believe that our education like such as South Africa and the Iraq, everywhere like such as, and I believe that they should our education over here, in the U.S., should help the U.S. or should help South Africa and should help the Iraq and the Asian countries so we will be able to build up our future for our," it made the news and the late-night comedy shows, and experienced instant YouTube fame. There were parodies, illustrated explanations, and responses from South Africans who thought that Miss Teen South Carolina shouldn't be trying to help them with their educations.[3]

It was as if collectively the nation had said, "Aha! We knew all along there was a downside to being that beautiful!"

Likewise, there is a serious downside to being a pretty. They're bubbleheads, stupid, only concerned with parties, clothes, and fitting in with their cliques. Their brain lesions make it hard for them to even think straight, let alone defy authority.

Even when Zane and Tally are trying to complete a simple task—looking for what is hidden in room 317 at the Valentino Mansion—they have to struggle just to keep their minds sharp. Later, they take calorie purgers so they're in a state of hunger and kiss each other to experience an adrenaline rush. After they're cured, they have to think of one terrifying stunt after another to keep the rest of the Crims bubbly. Shay and her clique resort to cutting themselves, since injury also sharpens their minds.

In our society—where we can't blame stupidity on doctor-implanted brain lesions—picking up a book is a much more effective route to escape stupidity. And if any impressionable pretty-young-

---

[3] And now when I ask my children a question to which they should know the answer but don't, like, "Where is your homework?" they look at me in the eye and say, "I believe that my homework like such as South Africa and the Iraq, everywhere like such as, and I believe. . . ." Yeah, it gets old.

things out there are reading the Uglies series, let me emphasize that climbing a transmission tower or crashing through an ice skating rink is really not the best way to add IQ points.

But here's one of those book club questions that will carry you through several chocolate chip cookies: Is the beautiful-but-stupid person a valid stereotype or just a bunch of sour grapes from the less-gorgeous masses? And if there is a correlation between beauty and stupidity, is it something people are born with or just a byproduct of the way good-looking people are treated?

Perhaps beautiful people learn from an early age that they don't have to develop their minds to gain acceptance from society. Why put in all that hard work learning and thinking, when everyone adores you just the way you are? Likewise, perhaps plainer people who are overlooked by their peers learn they must develop their minds in order to be appreciated.

Or maybe it's not a matter of what genetics assigns to us, but simply a matter of what people value. Perhaps smart people just value intelligence more than looks so they're less likely to spend time toning, tanning, buffing, bronzing, perming, primping, straightening, highlighting, eye-lining, lip glossing, nip-and-tucking, fashion shopping, and paying all the other dues of beauty. And people who value beauty—well, why waste time studying, reading, figuring, reflecting, hypothesizing, integrating, and educating when you already have a full schedule?

Or maybe the beautiful-but-stupid stereotype is only that: a stereotype, and a flawed one at that. After all, Brooke Shields—Calvin Klein model, actress, and the It Girl of the '80s—went to Princeton after she graduated from high school. Perhaps pretty people are just as smart as everyone else.

I refuse to offer my own opinion in this essay because I don't want readers to Google my name to see how attractive I am. I'll just move on to the next subject. (I will also start using big vocabulary words to prove my IQ is high.)

So how is it possible that we as a society want to be attractive, yet at the same time look down on beautiful people?

Scott Westerfeld addresses this subject (contradiction, dichotomy, inconsistency). Like the uglies looking at New Pretty Town, we tell ourselves that we wouldn't ever let looks affect our actions. We could be beautiful without the accompanying stupidity, selfishness, and shallow life. The uglies promise each other that they won't forget their friends once they turn pretty. They'll come back and visit their ugly friends. But they never do.

Is it as easy in our world to forget our ugly duckling roots? (Another good book club subject. Pass the cookies over here.)

Not only do the effects of beauty saturate the entire Uglies series, we are also able to see how beauty influences relationships—specifically Tally's, with David and Zane.

Out in the wilderness of the Smoke, Tally is able for the first time to see what normal people look like without the operation to turn them pretty. When she sees pictures in copies of old magazines she describes the people as freaks. She sees their bodies as grotesquely fat, weirdly over-muscled, or uncomfortably thin, and asks, "How could anyone stand to open their eyes?" (*Uglies*).

Shay tells Tally that if you keep looking, you get used to it, and Tally does. After a few days, she doesn't see David as a freak. She's attracted to his self-assurance, impressed by how he seems to know every step of every path intimately, and how he moves with effortless control. She thinks his eyes hold the same intensity of a cruel pretty but without any of their coldness (*Uglies*).

When David and Tally are alone together and he tells her he admires her, Tally trembles inside, and then realizes what she is feeling:

It was the same warmth she'd felt talking to Peris after his operation, or when teachers looked at her with approval. It was not a feeling she'd ever gotten from an ugly before. Without large, perfectly shaped eyes, their faces couldn't make you feel that way. But the moonlight and the setting, or maybe just the words he was saying, had somehow turned David into a pretty. (*Uglies*)

Tally can still see that his forehead is too high, that a small scar cuts a white stroke through his eyebrow, and that his smile is crooked. But something has changed inside Tally's head. She has learned that love has the power to make anyone look beautiful.

Tally overcomes the sway of evolution, and it's easy for the readers to feel the same way about David. He's so capable, thoughtful, and cool. Who wouldn't want a boyfriend like him? But then, we never actually see any characters' physical appearances in books.

Think of the ugliest guy you know. Now insert David's personality into his droopy eyes, pimply skin, chicken-bone arms, narrow-set eyes, and big nose. In real life, would you still want to date someone like David if he was, in fact, carrying around bucketfuls of ugly? Would it make any difference to you if you loved someone who all your friends thought scored rather high on the hideous scale?

It's easy to judge book characters on their merits alone when that's all we can see. Real life is harder.

In some ways I wish the story could have ended right there on page 250 of *Uglies* when Tally falls in love with David and sees him as beautiful. But it doesn't. Tally is turned into a pretty and, in the process, forgets about David and the things she's learned from and felt for him. She falls in love with Zane.

Just as it was with David, it isn't Zane's looks that make Tally love him. True, he's attractive, but so is everyone else. Zane is special and Tally realizes it. He's able to think his way out of being pretty-minded enough to realize what his city is doing to people on his own. Even before he met Tally, he was able to find ways to keep his mind clear. And when it comes time to take the cure, he is the one who is brave enough to take the untested pill and convinces Tally to do the same.

At the end of *Pretties*, when David tells Tally she just wants to stay with Zane because he's pretty, that it's evolution not rational thought that's influencing her, she answers,

> It's not the way Zane looks, David . . . it's because he makes me bubbly and because we took a lot of risks together. It could just as easily be me lying there, and he would stay with me if it was . . . it's because I love him.

Of course, Westerfeld does leave the reader questioning (hypothesizing, conjecturing, theorizing) whether this declaration is completely true, because in the last book of the trilogy, *Specials*, Tally has a different reaction to Zane. In her new role as a special, her senses have turned ultra sharp: "Everything was icy now, as if the world were opening her skin" (*Specials*). When Tally meets Zane after two months as a special, she can see him only as infirm, average, unspecial. Even the smell of his room makes her feel sick.

Shay and Tally tell Zane they'll help him to escape so that when he's captured he'll be turned into a special, and he and Tally can be together again.

> "Why can't we be together now?" he asked softly.
>
> Tally tried to imagine kissing his childlike lips, stroking his shaking hands, and the thought disgusted her.
>
> She shook her head. "I'm sorry . . . but not the way you are." (*Specials*)

After they leave Zane's apartment, Tally hates herself for feeling repulsed by the man she once loved and accuses Shay of knowing how seeing him would affect her. Shay answers, "I'm not the one in love. Haven't been since you stole David from me. But maybe I thought love might make a difference. Well, Tally-wa, did it make Zane special for you?"

Sadly, it doesn't. Love no longer has the power to make ugly things, like Zane's shaky movements, desirable in Tally's eyes. She asks, "What did Dr. Cable do to us, Shay? Do we have some kind of special lesions in our brains? Something that makes everyone else look pathetic? Like we're better than them?" (*Specials*).

Shay's answer—that they *are* better, and that everyone else looks confused and pitiful because they *are*—is good evidence that Shay either has brain lesions or has just been voted homecoming queen, one of the two.

But even with Tally's ability to rewire her mind and think herself free from lesions, she isn't able to truly love and appreciate Zane again until it's too late. In perhaps the saddest commentary on our desire for beauty and the lengths to which we'll go for it, Zane dies in an operation during an attack on Diego. He had hoped to be cured of his shakiness so Tally wouldn't see him as weak and average anymore. He believed, and rightly so, that if he was beautiful to her again, she would love him. Over and over again, Tally tells herself that his death is her fault, that "this was the final price of her massive ego" (*Specials*). It's easy to wish that Zane had opted out of the surgery, but can we really blame him for his decision? If given the choice, how many of us wouldn't risk a ten percent chance of dying in order to be breathtakingly beautiful, especially if being ugly was what stood between us and the person we loved?

Our plastic surgeons can't do nearly the job that the doctors in Westerfeld's novels do, but our society still has casualties in the quest for beauty. It's rare, but people occasionally do die during cosmetic surgery.

Less rare are the anorexics who ruin their health while trying to be thinner. And all too common are the people whose self-esteem withers away because they feel they'll never reach society's high standard of beauty. So many teens feel they will never be "good enough" because they don't look like the pictures of supermodels they constantly see in advertisements, magazines, TV—everywhere, really.

David says it best when he tells Tally, "That's the worst thing they do to you, to any of you. Whatever those brain lesions are all about, the worst damage is done before they even pick up the knife: you're all brainwashed into believing you're ugly."

It's fitting then that the story ends with the growth of the city of Diego, which is the opposite (antithesis, converse, conflicting parallel) of New Pretty Town. In Diego people get to choose their appearance. No standards seem to be set, and Tally sees different colors, face shapes, and even a bizarre surge where pinky fingers look like snakes. People are so accustomed to a wide assortment of features, in fact, that no one seems to pay much attention to Tally's special wolf-like beauty.

Along with this variety of looks comes a variety of opinions, and although there is disagreement in Diego, the reader is never left with the impression that this is a bad thing. It's simply the result of a multitude of people thinking different thoughts.

In Westerfeld's final comment on beauty at the end of *Specials*, Tally chooses not to change her appearance at all. (Although, really, I thought she should have at least changed her sharp, pointed teeth, which always reminded me of Little Red Riding Hood's big bad wolf.) It is as though Tally has finally come to the conclusion that her looks really don't matter.

David has also come to the same conclusion. After Tally escapes New Pretty Town and the two of them are talking about the future, David asks Tally if she is still a special.

> She gazed at him. "What do you think, David?"
> He peered into her eyes for a moment, then sighed and shook his head. "You just look like Tally to me."
> (*Specials*)

He's taken on five million years of evolution because his reaction to her is not influenced by how she looks.

And although she couldn't rewire herself in time to change how she felt about Zane's frailties, we know Tally's transformation is complete at the end of the story. She is no longer judging people by their looks.

When she was still a pretty and wanted David to abandon her, Tally screamed at him, "Get your ugly face out of here!" But at the end of *Specials* when she watches David, "her eyes cataloging all his imperfections, the asymmetry of his features, the pores of his skin, his too-big nose. His scar. He wasn't an ugly anymore: to her he was just David." I suppose that's how it works in our society too. On first appearance it's easy to judge people by their looks, to let evolution have its sway. After a while, though, friends and acquaintances no longer fall under the category of beautiful or ugly, but just look like themselves. Given time, the platitudes about beauty eventually come true and we really do pay attention to what's inside of people.

Comforting, yes, but that doesn't mean that all the issues we face with beauty don't take their toll on us in the meantime. If you still haven't decided whether you'd trade five years of your life to be beautiful, consider this: I realized one day, while I stood in front of the mirror getting ready to leave the house, that it was a trick question. Between showering, doing our hair, ironing clothes, and putting on makeup, we'll probably spend much more than five years of our lives trying to look beautiful.

---

Janette Rallison is the author of nine popular young adult novels, including *All's Fair in Love, War, and High School*, *It's a Mall World After All*, *Just One Wish*, and *My Fair Godmother*.

Janette has five children who keep her well supplied with plot ideas, sometimes even making cameo appearances in her novels. She likes to write romantic comedy because there is enough angst in real life, but there's a drastic shortage of both humor and romance.

# Conformity by Design

## Linda Gerber

As those of you who've read *Extras* may have guessed, I have an abiding interest in Japan. I studied the language in college, and read manga *ages* before it was cool. (You must believe me!) But Linda Gerber does one better: she was living in Japan while she read the Uglies series.

In a way, living in another culture is like reading science fiction—you're engaged in new ways of existing and of seeing that can wind up rewiring your brain. So perhaps it's not surprising that Gerber saw parallels between the dictates of Japanese society around her and those of Tally's city.

Join her in exploring how conformity and rebellion work together to build a culture, both in the U.S. and in Japan, and in the Uglies series. (And, as an added bonus, learn the secret meaning of "wa.")

SEVERAL YEARS AGO I lived in Tokyo, where I volunteered at our international school's library. It came to my attention that a book called *Uglies* was getting checked out. A lot. Once I tuned in to the title, I began to notice girls in the halls asking their friends if they'd read it yet. Naturally, my interest was piqued. I'm a book lover and always open to recommendations so, like a good little lemming, I put my name on the reserve list. When that wasn't fast enough, I ordered my own copy from Kinokuniya, one of the few bookstores in Tokyo to carry foreign titles.

At long last I got my hands on the book and quickly understood what the hype was about. I was sucked right into Tally's world and, living in Japan as I was at the time, understood a little too well the pressure she felt to be like everyone else. Conformity was also the rule in Japan, and I knew from experience the downsides of that rule.

The citizens of Tally's world are carefully programmed to accept a predetermined reality, their lives laid out in a pattern they are conditioned not to question. They move from littlies to school-housed uglies to partying pretties and finally to crumblies with no need to ponder the next step—or to think for themselves. Though Tally's society takes it to an extreme, I saw the same sort of indoctrinated pattern among my Japanese friends. They would study themselves dead from preschool through high school, often spending evenings and weekends in the Kumon study centers so they could get into the right university where it was widely accepted that, having achieved the goal of getting that college acceptance letter, they would party through the next few years. New Pretty Town, anyone? After college, it was time to get serious again and then join the ranks of salary-men—just like middle pretties—taking on more responsibility and bowing to the predetermined societal pattern.

In Japan, of course, dissenters are not hunted down and forced to submit as they are in Tally's world. There are no brain lesions to suppress individual thought. There is, however, a cultural expectation to conform that can be just as restricting. Reading the books, I felt a kinship with Shay and the others who long to break the mold and escape to the Smoke. I knew their anxiety of feeling trapped in a don't-be-different mindset.

In the United States, we have an old adage that says, "The squeaky wheel gets the grease." Japan has a similar saying with a much different take on that idea: "The nail that stands up gets beaten down." To simply things: Western society teaches that if you stand out or make enough noise, you'll eventually get what you want. Japanese culture says it's better to be the same and not draw attention to yourself.

Our family experienced this kind of conformity firsthand when my two youngest attended Japanese school. We quickly learned how imperative it was for them to be just like other kids if they wanted to fit in. Everything—and I mean *everything*—had to be the same: color of notebooks, type of pencils, brand of shoes. Students wore the same uniforms and carried the same hard-sided school back-pack—red for the girls and black for the boys. They all changed into the same kind of inside shoes at their identical lockers and ate their identical lunches from identical obento boxes. They even spoke in the same high-pitched, little child voices—especially the girls. My daughter actually changed the tone of her voice to fit in whenever she was around them.

Outside of the classroom as well, constant social programming was an inescapable part of life in Japan. Little cartoon signs hung throughout the train stations, reminding people how to think and act. Children were taught behavioral songs to sing. Even advertisements were geared to sell traditional Japanese values along with their products. Sound familiar? Yes, we do the same thing right here at home, although it may not be as obvious to us, since the values being fed to us are the ones we grew up with.

Social manipulation has a long and not-so-glorious history in American culture. Take a look at social engineering videos from the 1950s to see what I mean. These classroom classics preached about everything from respecting one's parents to personal hygiene to manners in school—often with ominous overtones for those who chose to ignore these important lessons. We may have come a long way since then, but we are far from free of more subtle forms of influence. There's big money to be made in advertising—convincing the public that a brand, politician, or lifestyle is desirable. Media promote certain ideas while disparaging others. Some new urban planning is even geared toward promoting specific lifestyle choices such as using green energy and patronizing local businesses.

Conspiracy theorists might see some nefarious purpose behind all this propaganda and engineering, but my guess is that it starts off rather innocently. Someone believes that their set of ideals and values are important enough that everyone should see things their way. They probably think the world would be a better place if we were all the same. But would it?

In *Uglies*, we saw a rather stark example of the destructive potential of sameness: the encroachment of the white tiger orchid. The orchid was engineered, with the best of intentions, to thrive in any environment. The result was that it became the perfect weed, taking over entire forests, choking out the other vegetation so that there was nothing left to replenish the soil, provide shade, or resist drought or disease. Eventually the orchids died off and left only barren land in their wake. In nature as in society, monoculture—everything the same—eventually leads to a "biological zero." Without diversity, nothing survives.

And yet . . .

I have to admit that in Japan, that same conformity I found so confining had benefits as well. In a society where space is at a premium and privacy is non-existent, working together for the greater good makes a lot of sense. Under those circumstances, supreme cooperation is needed in order for people to peacefully coexist.

And so, despite the message of individuality that I wholeheartedly embraced in the books, I could see in the society around me that some conformity could actually be a Good Thing.

Yeah, I know what you're thinking. We all saw what enforced conformity did to Tally's society. But that's the point. Not all societies and cultures are the same. In our Western world, we are taught to value individuality, but many Asian cultures such as Japan value sameness in pursuit of social harmony.

Which philosophy is better? With conformity, a society runs more efficiently and maintains its current state, but with individuality, the encouragement of new ideas advances society (or pulls it back, depending on the idea). With conformity comes peaceful living and with individualism comes cultural productivity. Both offer desirable—though different—outcomes. In the words of philosopher Friedrich Nietzsche, "You have your way. I have my way. As for the right way, the correct way, and the only way, it does not exist." Perhaps the best we can hope for is to appreciate the value of each point of view.

To understand the conformist philosophy, you need to look at the underlying values on which it's based. In Japan, these values are deeply imbedded in the Shinto beliefs, which value group solidarity more than individual identity. Traditionally, the most important social value is *wa*, or harmony. The welfare of the majority comes first. Thoughts for oneself are considered shallow and selfish. One who is enlightened would let go of their individual needs out of respect for the society as a whole.

This is not to say that the Japanese don't have their own individual thoughts, fears, and desires like everyone else. They do, but they learn to distinguish between their *hone* (their true feelings) and their *tatemai* (the face they wear in public). If their *hone* goes against the harmony of the group, they are expected to rise above their own selfish feelings and "put on a good face" for the benefit of the group.

(This concept of "face" was especially interesting to consider while reading *Extras*. . . .)

Compared to our me-first Western culture, this kind of philosophy may seem a bit confining, but social harmony does have its advantages. For one thing, you always know what is expected of you and what you can expect from others. That lends a sense of community and safety unheard of in Western countries. For example, one of the things that shocked me when I first arrived in Japan was to see little pre-school kids riding trains and busses *unaccompanied*. They wore little yellow caps and yellow flaps on their backpacks, which identified them as the youngest of all school-aged children, and adults—even complete strangers—would take special care to watch out for them and ensure their safety.

With this kind of community also comes a sense of belonging that helps to define who you are as an individual. And it's not unique to Asian cultures.

In the States, people join clubs and societies seeking this same benefit of belonging. Each member benefits from the power of the group, and conforming to the group's rules and restrictions is the price paid for that power.

Agreeing to conform isn't always a bad thing. Members of sports teams, for example, purposefully work to think and act alike. They even dress the same, their team uniforms presenting them as a cohesive Group rather than a bunch of Individuals. Fans of these teams often clothe themselves similarly, which gives them a sense of pride and belonging (especially if their team is winning).

I currently live in the shadows of Ohio State University. This is Buckeye country through and through, and the community comes together each week in support of the scarlet and gray. It's a great unifier; the same Buckeye flags hang over the garages of the million-dollar homes in Muirfield and the duplexes in South Columbus. People from all walks of life wear OSU jerseys and sweatshirts to show their solidarity. Even local business owners get in on the action, proclaiming their loyalty to the team. It gives the businesses a "we're all in this together" edge. It's hard to see a downside in that.

Many schools enforce a certain amount of conformity to ensure an effective learning environment for their students. Students learn that for the good of the group, certain behavior is not allowed. They are expected to perform to a set standard. Some schools even choose to enforce a dress code or issue school uniforms to promote equality among students.

Similarly, professional guilds and organizations set forth bylaws that all members must conform to in order to retain their membership. Doing so sets a standard within their profession by which they can be held accountable.

Even for the rebels of the Uglies books, conformity has its place. For example, the Smokies, living in the wilderness as they do, depend on each other for survival. They establish a society complete with a bartering system and work assignments. All members of the society have to cooperate within this framework for it to work. Even one dissenter among the ranks could be dangerous, as they find out after Tally gets there.

And although Dr. Cable had convinced Tally to betray Shay and locate the Smoke, notice how Tally changes her outlook once she arrives. She conforms to the expectations of her new society so that she can fit in. True, she has an ulterior motive at first, but her interest in David and eventually her desire to be part of the group allows her to reset the programming she had received for sixteen years and to see things from a completely different perspective.

Notice also that it takes individual thought for her to decide to conform to the needs of her new society; it is her choice. Free will. That was the main difference I could see between the conformist society I witnessed in Japan and the world Tally and Shay face in Uglyville. In Japan it may be frowned upon to buck the system. It might cost job opportunities and social status. But ultimately the option exists to make that choice. Make one visit to the popular teen hangout in Harajuku and you can see that plenty of young people have chosen to express their individuality. In Tally and Shay's society, however, no choice is offered. Whether they like it or not, they must conform.

Worse, giving in to the system meant quite literally that they would lose their individuality. Not only would they be made to look like everyone else, but the lesions on their brains would rob them of their free will, making them pliable and controllable. This is where the Powers That Be so often go completely and utterly wrong. Even with socialism and communism, the underlying philosophies come from a sincere desire to even the playing field—to be equal and fair to all members of society. But the moment a person is forced against his or her will to submit to the system, the philosophy fails, because it means one person's will is being valued above another's. Equity goes out the window when some people are just a little more "equal" than others and are able to make decisions for the masses without consent and without recourse. As British historian and moralist John Emerich Edward Dalberg Acton noted, "Power tends to corrupt, and absolute power corrupts absolutely."

Even if the Powers That Be in Tally's world originally believed they were doing the right thing—protecting the world from another collapse and creating a society wherein everyone would be treated as equals—they lost their white hats the moment they resorted to brainwashing and compulsory plastic surgery. They were doing with social conditioning and brain lesions what Stalin did with propaganda and enforced ignorance—removing the power of the individual to think for him- or herself.

But really, was all that robbing of power necessary? Given the choice, would people really choose not to conform? The answer is yes . . . and no. While there may be some true individualists among us, most of us choose to follow the group in one way or another. As the ancient Greek playwright Euripides said, "No man on earth is truly free. All are slaves of money or necessity. Public opinion or fear of prosecution forces each one, against his conscience, to conform." Amazing how so little has changed in over two thousand years. Euripides is said to have lived about 485–406 B.C., far removed from the technology and communication we enjoy today—and yet the same pressure to conform he talked about then still exists. Even those who would like to believe they are being unique often fall in with a group of conforming non-conformists. They may be different than the majority, but they still seek approval and acceptance from their own group.

In the Uglies books, we see this after the mind-rain and the fall of the oppressive regime. A surprising number of people still choose to receive the pretty operation, even when it is no longer mandated Finally given the opportunity to be as individual as they want to be, they still choose to carve themselves into what they believe is desirable to the society as a whole. No longer part of the simple division of uglies and pretties, people choose to divide into cliques or groups and to adjust themselves to fit into the new group's identity: Crims, Radical Honesty, Cutters, etc. Even the Sly Girls are conformists of a sort, although it could be argued that they are perhaps the least conforming of the groups because they choose to remain anonymous, not seeking approval from society but only from each other. But since they *do* depend on approval from each other to fit in with the group, I'm including them with the elective conformists. When given a choice, they choose to belong.

In the end, that might be the important distinction, not conformity versus individuality, but choice versus no choice. As I saw it, that was why it is so important to Maddy and Az that they discover a cure for the lesions, and why Tally and the other Smokies are willing to risk so much to warn the others back in the city. Knowledge, as it turns out, really is power.

That's one lesson we can learn from Tally's story: No matter where we live, be it Tokyo or Uglyville, we can design our own futures by being aware of the influences that lead us to live, act, or think a certain way instead of blindly following. We may still choose conformity, but only if that is what we believe is best for us. After all, that's what being an individual is all about.

---

Linda Gerber is the non-conforming author of the YA mysteries *Death by Bikini*, *Death by Latte*, and *Death by Denim*. She currently lives and writes in Dublin, Ohio, blissfully ignoring her husband, kids, and one very naughty puppy.

# The Beautiful People

## Charles Beaumont

Beauty and appearance have been themes of science fiction for a long time. Writers have imagined worlds where everyone is beautiful, or looks exactly the same, or where strict standards of averageness are enforced. Here in Charles Beaumont's "The Beautiful People" we have a classic of the sub-genre. The story was written in 1952, proving that our obsession with cosmetic surgery goes back farther than you might think. Uglies fans will certainly recognize its fundamental setting—a society in which conformity begins with a perfect face. But I'll leave it to you to tease out the other similarities and differences between Tally's world and Mary's.

As many of you know, the story was adapted by John Tomerlin in 1964 as a *Twilight Zone* episode, "Number 12 Looks Just Like You." That episode began with these words: "Given the chance, what young girl wouldn't happily exchange a plain face for a lovely one? What girl could refuse the opportunity to be beautiful?" Maybe that's the question I wanted to answer.

MARY SAT QUIETLY AND watched the handsome man's legs blown off, watched on further as the great ship began to crumple and break into small pieces in the middle of the blazing night. She fidgeted slightly as the men and the parts of the men came floating dreamily through the wreckage out into the awful silence. And when the meteorite shower came upon the men, flying in gouging holes through everything, tearing flesh and ripping bones, Mary closed her eyes.

"Mother."

Mrs. Cuberle glanced up from her magazine.

"Do we have to wait much longer?"

"I don't think so, why?"

Mary said nothing but looked at the moving wall.

"Oh, that." Mrs. Cuberle laughed and shook her head. "That tired old thing. Read a magazine, Mary, like I'm doing. We've all seen *that* a million times."

"Does it have to be on, Mother?"

"Well, nobody seems to be watching. I don't think the doctor would mind if I switched it off."

Mrs. Cuberle rose from the couch and walked to the wall. She depressed a little button and the life went from the wall, flickering and glowing.

Mary opened her eyes.

"Honestly," Mrs. Cuberle said to the woman beside her, "you'd think they'd try to get something else. We might all as well go to the museum and watch the first landing on Mars. The Mayorka Disaster—really!"

The woman replied without distracting her eyes from the magazine page. "It's the doctor's idea. Psychological."

Mrs. Cuberle opened her mouth and moved her head up and down, knowingly. "I should have known there was *some* reason. Still, who watches it?"

"The children do. Makes them think, makes them grateful or something."

"Oh. Of course, yes."

"Psychological."

Mary picked up a magazine and leafed through the pages. All photographs, of women and men. Women like Mother and like the others in the room; slender, tanned, shapely, beautiful women; and men with large muscles and shiny hair. Women and men, all looking alike, all perfect and beautiful. She folded the magazine and wondered how to answer the questions that would be asked.

"Mother—"

"Gracious, what is it now! Can't you sit still for a minute?"

"But we've been here three hours."

Mrs. Cuberle sniffed.

"Do I really have to?"

"Now, don't be silly, Mary. After those terrible things you told me, of *course* you do."

An olive-skinned woman in a transparent white uniform came into the reception room.

"Cuberle. Mrs. Zena Cuberle?"

"Yes."

"Doctor will see you now."

Mrs. Cuberle took Mary's hand and they walked behind the nurse down a long corridor.

A man who seemed in his middle twenties looked up from a desk. He smiled and gestured towards two adjoining chairs.

"Well, well."

"Doctor Hortel, I—"

The doctor snapped his fingers.

"Of course, I know. Your daughter. Well, I know your trouble. Get so many of them nowadays, takes up most of my time."

"You do?" asked Mrs. Cuberle. "Frankly, it had begun to upset me."

"Upset? Hmm. Not good at all. But then—if people did not get upset, then we psychiatrists would be out of a job, eh? Go the way of the M.D. But I assure you, I need hear no more."

He turned his handsome face to Mary. "Little girl, how old are you?"

"Eighteen, sir."

"Oh, a real bit of impatience. It's just about time, of course. What might your name be?"

"Mary."

"Charming! and so unusual. Well, now, Mary, may I say that I understand your problem—understand it thoroughly."

Mrs. Cuberle smiled and smoothed the metalwork on her jerkin.

"Madam, you have no idea how many there are these days. Sometimes it preys on their minds so that it affects them physically, even mentally. Makes them act strange, say peculiar, unexpected things. One little girl I recall was so distraught she did nothing but brood all day long. Can you imagine!"

"That's what Mary does. When she finally told me, Doctor, I thought she had gone—you know."

"That bad, eh? Afraid we'll have to start a re-education program, very soon, or they'll all be like this. I believe I'll suggest it to the Senator day after tomorrow."

"I don't quite understand, Doctor."

"Simply, Mrs. Cuberle, that the children have got to be thoroughly instructed. Thoroughly. Too much is taken for granted and childish minds somehow refuse to accept things without definite reason. Children have become far too intellectual, which, as I trust I needn't remind you, is a dangerous thing."

"Yes, but what has this to do with—"

"Mary, like half the sixteen-, seventeen- and eighteen-year-olds today, has begun to feel acutely self-conscious. She feels that her body has developed sufficiently for the Transformation—which of course it has not, not quite yet—and she cannot understand the complex reasons which compel her to wait until some vague, though specific, date. Mary looks at you, at the women all about her, at the pictures, and then she looks into a mirror. From pure perfection of body, face, limbs, pigmentation, carriage, stance, she sees herself and is horrified. Isn't that so? Of course. She asks herself, 'Why must I be hideous, unbalanced, oversize, undersize, full of revolting skin eruption, badly schemed organic arrangements?'—in short, Mary is tired of being a monster and is overly anxious to achieve what almost everyone else has already achieved."

"But—" said Mrs. Cuberle.

"This much you understand, doubtless. Now, Mary, what you object to is that our society offers you, and the others like you, no convincing logic on the side of waiting until nineteen. It is all taken for granted and you want to know why! It is that simple. A non-technical explanation will not suffice. The modern child wants facts, solid technical data, to satisfy her every question. And that, as you can both see, will take a good deal of reorganizing."

"But—" said Mary.

"The child is upset, nervous, tense; she acts strange, peculiar, odd, worries you and makes herself ill because it is beyond our meager powers to put it across. I tell you, what we need is a whole new basis for learning. And, that will take doing. It will take *doing*, Mrs. Cuberle. Now, don't you worry about Mary, and don't you worry, child. I'll prescribe some pills and—"

"No, no, Doctor! You're all mixed up," cried Mrs. Cuberle.

"I *beg* your pardon, Madam?"

"What I mean is, you've got it wrong. Tell him, Mary, tell the doctor what you told me."

Mary shifted uneasily in the chair.

"It's that—I don't want it."

The doctor's well-proportioned jaw dropped.

"Would you please repeat that?"

"I said, I don't want the Transformation."

"But that's impossible. I have never heard of such a thing. Little girl, you are playing a joke."

Mary nodded negatively.

"See, Doctor. What can it be?" Mrs. Cuberle rose and began to pace.

The doctor clucked his tongue and took from a small cupboard a black box covered with buttons and dials and wire. He affixed black clamps to Mary's head.

"Oh no, you don't think—I mean, could it?"

"We shall soon see." The doctor revolved a number of dials and studied the single bulb in the centre of the box. It did not flicker. He removed the clamps.

"Dear me," the doctor said. "Your daughter is perfectly sane, Mrs. Cuberle."

"Well, then what is it?"

"Perhaps she is lying. We haven't completely eliminated that factor as yet, it slips into certain organisms."

More tests. More machines, and more negative results.

Mary pushed her foot in a circle on the floor. When the doctor put his hands to her shoulders she looked up pleasantly.

"Little girl," said the handsome man, "do you actually mean to tell us that you *prefer* that body?"

"I like it. It's—hard to explain, but it's me and that's what I like. Not the looks, maybe, but the *me*."

"You can look in the mirror and see yourself, then look at—well, at your mother and be content?"

"Yes, sir." Mary thought of her reasons; fuzzy, vague, but very definitely there. Maybe she had said the reason. No. Only a part of it.

"Mrs. Cuberle," the doctor said, "I suggest that your husband have a long talk with Mary."

"My husband is dead. The Ganymede incident."

"Oh, splendid. Rocket man, eh? Very interesting organisms. Something always seems to happen to rocket men, in one way or another." The doctor scratched his cheek. "When did she first start talking this way?" he asked.

"Oh, for quite some time. I used to think it was because she was such a baby. But lately, the time getting so close and all, I thought I'd better see you."

"Of course, yes, very wise, uh—does she also do odd things?"

"Well, I found her on the second level one night. She was lying on the floor, and when I asked her what she was doing, she said she was trying to sleep."

Mary flinched. She was sorry, in a way, that Mother had found that out.

"Did you say 'sleep'?"

"That's right."

"Now where could she have picked that up?"

"No idea."

"Mary, don't you know nobody sleeps anymore. That we have an infinitely greater life-span than our poor ancestors now that that wasteful state of unconsciousness has been conquered? Child, have you actually *slept*? No one knows how anymore."

"No, sir, but I almost did."

The doctor breathed a long stream of air from his mouth.

"But, how could you begin to try to do something people have forgotten entirely about?"

"The way it was described in the book, it sounded nice, that's all."

"Book, book? Are there *books* at your Unit, Madam?"

"There could be. I haven't cleaned up in a while."

"That is certainly peculiar. I haven't seen a book for years. Not since '17."

Mary began to fidget and stare nervously.

"But with the Tapes, why should you try to read books. . . . Where did you get them?"

"Daddy did. He got them from his father and so did Grandpa. He said they're better than the Tapes and he was right."

Mrs. Cuberle flushed.

"My husband was a little strange, Doctor Hortel. He kept these things despite anything I said. Finally hid them, as I see."

The muscular black-haired doctor walked to another cabinet and selected from the shelf a bottle. From the bottle he took two large pills and swallowed these.

"Sleep . . . books . . . doesn't want the Transformation . . . Mrs. Cuberle, my *dear* good woman, this is grave. I would appreciate it if you would change psychiatrists. I am very busy and, ah, this is somewhat specialized. I suggest Central-dome. Many fine doctors there. Goodbye."

The doctor turned and sat in a large chair and folded his hands. Mary watched him and wondered why the simple statements should have so changed things. But the doctor did not move from the chair.

"Well!" said Mrs. Cuberle and walked quickly from the room.

Mary considered the reflection in the mirrored wall. She sat on the floor and looked at different angles of herself: profile, full-face, full-length, naked, clothed. Then she took up the magazine and studied it. She sighed.

"Mirror, Mirror on the wall. . . ." The words came haltingly to her mind and from her lips. She hadn't read these, she recalled. Daddy had said them, "quoted" them as he put it. But they too were lines from a book. ". . . who is the fairest of—"

A picture of Mother sat upon the dresser and Mary considered this now. She looked for a long time at the slender feminine neck, knotted in just the right places. The golden skin, smooth and without blemish, without wrinkles and without age. The dark brown eyes and the thin tapers of eyebrows, the long black lashes. Set evenly, so that the halves of the face corresponded precisely. The half-hearted mouth, a violet tint against the gold, the white teeth, even, sparkling.

Mother, Beautiful, Transformed Mother. And back again to the mirror.

"—of them all. . . ."

The image of a rather chubby young woman, without lines of rhythm of grace, without perfection. Splotchy skin full of little holes, puffs in the cheeks, red eruptions on the forehead. Perspiration, shapeless hair flowing onto shapeless shoulders down a shapeless body. Like all of them, before the Transformation. . . .

Did they *all* look like this, before? Did Mother, even?

Mary thought hard, trying to sort out exactly what Daddy and Grandpa had said, why they said the Transformation was a bad thing, and why she believed and agreed with them so strongly. It made little sense, but they were right. They *were* right! And one day, she would understand completely.

Mrs. Cuberle slammed the door angrily and Mary jumped to her feet.

"Honestly, expenses aren't so high that you have to leave all the windows off. I went through the whole level and there isn't a single window left on. Don't you even want to see the people?"

"No. I was thinking."

"Well, it's got to stop. It's simply got to stop. Mary, what in the world has gotten into you lately?"

"I—"

"The way you upset Doctor Hortel. He won't even see me

anymore, and these traumas are getting horrible—*not* to mention the migraines. I'll have to get that awful Doctor Wagoner."

Mrs. Cuberle sat on the couch and crossed her legs carefully.

"And what in the world were you doing on the floor?"

"Trying to sleep."

"You've got to stop talking that way! Why should you want to do such a silly thing?"

"The books—"

"And you mustn't read those terrible things."

"Mother—"

"The Unit is full of Tapes, full! Anything you want!"

Mary stuck out her lower lip. "But I don't want to hear all about wars and colonizations and politics!"

"Now I know where you got this idiotic notion that you don't want the Transformation. Of *course*."

Mrs. Cuberle rose quickly and took the books from the corner and from the closet and piled her arms with them. She looked everywhere in the room and gathered the old brittle volumes.

These she carried from the room and threw into the elevator. A button guided the doors shut.

"I thought you'd do that," Mary said, slowly, "that's why I hid most of the good ones. Where you'll never find them!" She breathed heavily and her heart thumped.

Mrs. Cuberle put a satin handkerchief to her eyes.

"I don't know what I ever did to deserve this!"

"Deserve *what*, Mother? What am I doing that's so wrong?" Mary's mind rippled in a little confused stream now.

"What?" Mrs. Cuberle wailed, "*What?* Do you think I want people to point at you and say I'm the mother of a mutant?" Her voice softened abruptly into a plea. "Or have you changed your mind, dear?"

"No." *The vague reasons, longing to be put into words.*

"It really doesn't hurt, you know. They just take off a little skin and put some on and give you pills and electronic treatment and things like that. It doesn't take more than a week."

"No." *The reasons.*

"Look at your friend Shala, she's getting her Transformation next month. And *she's* almost pretty now."

"Mother, I don't care—"

"If it's the bones you're worried about, well, that doesn't hurt. They give you a shot and when you wake up, everything's molded right. Everything, to suit the personality."

"I don't care, I don't care."

"But *why?*"

"I like me the way I am." *Almost, almost exactly. But not quite. Part of it, though; part of what Daddy and Grandpa must have meant.*

Mrs. Cuberle switched on a window and then switched it off again. She sobbed. "But you're so ugly, dear! Like Doctor Hortel said. And Mr. Willmes, at the factor. He told some people he thought you were the ugliest girl he'd ever seen. He says he'll be thankful when you have your Transformation."

"Daddy said I was beautiful."

"Well, really, dear. You *do* have eyes."

"Daddy said that real beauty is more than skin deep. He said a lot of things like that and when I read the books I felt the same way. I guess I don't want to look like everybody else, that's all."

"You'll notice that your father had *his* Transformation, though!"

Mary stamped her foot angrily. "He told me that if he had to do it again he just wouldn't. He said I should be stronger than he was."

"You're not going to get away with this, young lady. After all, I *am* your mother."

A bulb flickered in the bathroom and Mrs. Cuberle walked uncertainly to the cabinet. She took out a little cardboard box.

"It's time for lunch."

Mary nodded. That was another thing the books talked about, which the Tapes did not. Lunch seemed to be something special long ago, or at least different . . . The books talked of strange ways of putting a load of things into the mouth and chewing this things. Enjoying them, somehow. Strange and wonderful. . . .

"And you'd better get ready for work."

Mary let the greenish capsule slide down her throat.

"Yes, Mother."

The office was quiet and without shadows. The walls gave off a steady luminescence, distributing the light evenly upon all the desks and tables. It was neither hot nor cold.

Mary held the ruler firmly and allowed the pen to travel down the metal edge effortlessly. The new black lines were small and accurate. She tipped her head, compared the notes beside her to the plan she was working on. She noticed the beautiful people looking at her more furtively than before, and she wondered about this as she made her lines.

A tall man rose from his desk in the rear of the office and walked down the aisle to Mary's table. He surveyed her work, allowing his eyes to travel cautiously from her face to the draft.

Mary looked around.

"Nice job," said the man.

"Thank you, Mr. Willmes."

"Dralich shouldn't have anything to complain about. That crane should hold the whole damn city."

"It's very good alloy, sir."

"Yeah. Say, kid, you got a minute?"

"Yes, sir."

"Let's go into Mullinson's office."

The big handsome man led the way into a small cubbyhole of a room. He motioned to a chair and sat on the edge of one desk.

"Kid, I never was one to beat around the bush. Somebody called in a little while ago, gave me some crazy story about you not wanting your Transformation."

Mary looked away, then quickly back into the man's eyes. "It's not a crazy story, Mr. Willmes," she said. "It's true. I want to stay this way."

The man stared, then coughed embarrassedly.

"What the hell—excuse me, kid, but—I don't exactly get it. You ain't a mutant, I know that. And you ain't—"

"Insane? No; Doctor Hortel can tell you."

The man laughed, nervously. "Well. . . . Look, you're still a cub, but you do swell work. Lots of good results, lots of comments from the stations. But Mr. Poole won't like it."

"I know. I know what you mean, Mr. Willmes. But nothing can change my mind."

"You'll get old before you're half through life!"

Yes, she would. Old, like the Elders, wrinkled and brittle, unable to move correctly. Old.

"It's hard to make you understand. But I don't see why it should make any difference, as long as I do my work."

"Now don't go getting me wrong, kid. It ain't me. But you know, I don't run Interplan. I just work here. Mr. Poole, he likes things running smooth and it's my job to carry it out. And as soon as everybody finds out, things wouldn't run smooth. There'll be a big to-do, y'understand? The dames will start asking questions and talk. Be the same as a mutant in the office—no offense."

"Will you accept my resignation, then, Mr. Willmes?"

"Sure you won't change your mind?"

"No, sir. I decided that a long time ago."

"Well, then, I'm sorry, Mary. Couple, ten, twenty years you could be centraled on one of the asteroids, the way you been working out. But . . . if you should change your mind, there'll always be a job for you here. Otherwise, you got till March. And between you and me, I hope by then you've decided the other way."

Mary walked back down the aisle, past the rows of desks. Past the men and women. The handsome model men and the beautiful, perfect women, perfect, all perfect, all looking alike. Looking exactly alike.

She sat down again and took up her ruler and pen.

Mary stepped into the elevator and descended several hundred feet. At the Second Level she pressed a button and the elevator stopped. The doors opened with another button and the doors to her Unit with still another.

Mrs. Cuberle sat on the floor by the TV, disconsolate and red-eyed. Her blonde hair had come slightly askew and a few strands hung over her forehead.

"You don't need to tell me. No one will hire you."

Mary sat down beside her mother.

"If only you hadn't told Mr. Willmes in the first place—"

"Well, I thought *he* could beat a little sense into you."

The sounds from the TV grew louder. Mrs. Cuberle changed channels a number of times and finally turned it off.

"What did you do today, Mother?" Mary smiled, hopefully.

"What *can* I do now? Nobody will even come over! Everyone thinks you're a mutant."

"*Mother!*"

"They say you should be in the Circuses."

Mary went into another room. Mrs. Cuberle followed, wringing her hands, and crying: "Mutant, mutant! How are we going to live? Where does the money come from now? Next thing they'll be firing *me*!"

"No one would do that."

"Nobody else on this planet has ever refused the Transformation. The mutants all wish they could have it. And you, given everything, you turn it down. You *want* to be ugly!"

Mary put her arms about her mother's shoulders.

"I wish I could explain; I've tried so hard to. It isn't that I want to bother anyone, or that Daddy or Grandpa wanted me to."

Mrs. Cuberle reached into the pocket of her jerkin and retrieved a purple pill. She swallowed the pill.

When the letter dropped from the chute, Mrs. Cuberle ran to snatch it up. She read it once silently, then smiled.

"Oh," she said, "I was so afraid they wouldn't answer. But we'll see about this *now*!"

She gave the letter to Mary, who read:

Mrs. Zena Cuberle
Unit 451-D
Levels II & III
City

Dear Madam:

In re your letter of Dec. 3 36. We have carefully examined your complaint and consider that it requires stringent measures of some sort. Quite frankly, the possibility of such a complaint has never occurred to this Dept. and we therefore cannot issue positive directives at this present moment.

However, due to the unusual qualities of the matter, we have arranged an audience at Centraldome 8th level 16th Unit, Jan. 3 37, 23 sharp. Dr. Hortel has been instructed to attend. You will bring the subject in question.

Yrs.
DEPT. F

Mary let the paper flutter to the floor. She walked quietly to the elevator and set it for Level III. When the elevator stopped, she ran from it, crying, into her room.

She thought and remembered and tried to sort out and put together. Daddy had said it, Grandpa had, the books did. Yes. The books did.

She read until her eyes burned and her eyes burned until she could read no more. Then Mary went to sleep, softly and without realizing it.

But the sleep was not a peaceful one.

"Ladies and gentlemen," said the young-looking, classic-featured man, "this problem does not resolve easily. Doctor Hortel here, testifies that Mary Cuberle is definitely not insane, Doctors Monagh, Prynn, and Fedders all verify this judgment. Doctor Prynn asserts that the human organism is no longer so constructed as to create and sustain such an attitude as deliberate falsehood. Further, there is positively nothing in the structure of Mary Cuberle which might suggest difficulties in Transformation. There is qualified evidence for all these statements. And yet—" the man sighed "—while the Newstapes, the Foto services, while every news-carrying agency has circulated this problem throughout the universe, we are faced with this refusal. Further, the notoriety has become excessive to the point of vulgarity and has resultantly caused numerous persons, among them Mrs. Zena Cuberle, the child's mother, grievous emotional stress. What, may I ask, is to be done therefore?"

Mary looked at a metal table.

"We have been in session far too long, holding up far too many other pressing contingencies of a serious nature."

Throughout the rows of beautiful people, the mumbling increased. Mrs. Cuberle sat nervously tapping her foot and running a comb through her hair.

"The world waits," continued the man. "Mary Cuberle, you have been given innumerable chances to reconsider, you know."

Mary said, "I know. But I don't want to."

The beautiful people looked at Mary and laughed. Some shook their heads.

The man in the robes threw up his hands.

"Little girl, can you realize what an issue you have caused? The unrest, the wasted time? Do you fully understand what you have done? We could send you to a Mutant Colony, I suppose you know. . . ."

"How could you do that?" inquired Mary.

"Well, I'm sure we could—it's a pretty point. Intergalactic questions hang fire while you sit there saying the same thing over and over. And in judicial procedure I dare say there is some clause which forbids that. Come now, doesn't the happiness of your dear mother mean anything to you? Or your duty to the state to the entire Solar System?"

A slender, supple woman in a back row stood and cried, loudly: "*Do* something!"

The man on the high stool raised his arm.

"None of that, now. We must conform, even though the problem is out of the ordinary."

The woman sat down, snorted; the man turned again to Mary.

"Child, I have here a petition, signed by two thousand individuals and representing all the Stations of the Earth. They have been made aware of all the facts and have submitted the petition voluntarily. It's all so unusual and I'd hoped we wouldn't have to—but, well the petition urges drastic measures."

The mumbling rose.

"The petition urges that you shall, upon final refusal, be forced by law to accept the Transformation. And that an act of legislature shall make this universal and binding in the future."

Mary's eyes were open, wide; she stood and paused before speaking.

"*Why?*" she asked.

The man in the robes passed a hand through his hair.

Another voice from the crowd: "Sign the petition, Senator!"

All the voices: "Sign it! Sign it!"

"But *why?*" Mary began to cry. The voices stilled for a moment.

"Because—Because—What if others should get the same idea? What would happen to us then, little girl? We'd be right back to the ugly, thin, fat, unhealthy-looking race we were ages ago! There can't be any exceptions."

"Maybe they didn't consider themselves so ugly!"

The mumbling began anew and broke into a wild clamour.

"That isn't the point," cried the man in the robes, "you *must* conform!"

And the voices cried "Yes!" loudly until the man took up a pen and signed the papers on his desk.

Cheers; applause; shouts.

Mrs. Cuberle patted Mary on the top of her head.

"There now!" she said happily, "everything will be all right now. You'll see, Mary, dear."

The Transformation Parlor covered the entire Level, sprawling with its departments. It was always filled and there was nothing to sign and no money to pay and people were always waiting in line.

But today the people stood aside. And there were still more, looking in through doors, TV cameras placed throughout and Tape machines in every corner. It was filled, but not bustling as usual.

The Transformation Parlor was terribly quiet.

Mary walked past the people, Mother and the men in back of her, following. She looked at the people, too, as she did in her room through turned-on windows. It was no different. The people were beautiful, perfect, without a single flaw. Except the young ones, young like herself, seated on couches, looking embarrassed and ashamed and eager.

But, of course, the young ones did not count.

All the beautiful people. All the ugly people, staring out from bodies that were not theirs. Walking on legs that had been made for them, laughing with manufactured voices, gesturing with shaped and fashioned arms.

Mary walked slowly despite the prodding. In her eyes, in *her* eyes, was a mounting confusion; a wide, wide wonderment.

She looked down at her own body, then at the walls which reflected it. Flesh of her flesh, bone of her bone, all hers, made by no person, built by herself or Someone she did not know. . . . Uneven kneecaps making two grinning cherubs when they straightened, and the old familiar rubbing together of fat inner thighs. Fat, unshapely, unsystematic Mary. But *Mary.*

Of course. Of course! This *was* what Daddy meant, what Grandpa and the books meant. What *they* would know if they would read the books or hear the words, the good, unreasonable words, the words that signified more, so much more, than any of this. . . .

"Where *are* these people?" Mary said, half to herself. "What has happened to *them* and don't they miss *themselves*, these manufactured things?"

She stopped, suddenly.

"Yes! That *is* the reason. They have all forgotten themselves!"

A curvaceous woman stepped forward and took Mary's hand. The woman's skin was tinted dark. Chipped and sculptured bone into slender rhythmic lines, electrically created carriage, made, turned out. . . .

"All right, young lady. Shall we begin?"

They guided Mary to a large, curved leather seat.

From the top of a long silver pole a machine lowered itself. Tiny bulbs glowed to life and cells began to click. The people stared. Slowly a picture formed upon the screen in the machine. Bulbs directed at Mary, then re-directed into themselves. Wheels turning, buttons ticking.

The picture was completed.

"Would you like to see it?"

Mary closed her eyes, tight.

"It's really very nice." The woman turned to the crowd. "Oh yes, there's a great deal to be salvaged; you'd be surprised. A great deal. We'll keep the nose and I don't believe the elbows will have to be altered at all."

Mrs. Cuberle looked at Mary and grinned.

"Now, it isn't so bad as you thought, is it?" she said.

The beautiful people looked. Cameras turned, Tapes wound.

"You'll have to excuse us now. Only the machines allowed."

*Only the machines.*

The people filed out, grumbling.

Mary saw the rooms in the mirror. Saw things in the rooms, the faces and bodies that had left, the woman and the machines and the old young men standing about, adjusting, readying.

Then she looked at the picture in the screen.

A woman of medium height stared back at her. A woman with a curved body and thin legs; silver hair, pompadoured, cut short; full sensuous lips, small breasts, flat stomach, unblemished skin.

A strange woman no one had ever seen before.

The nurse began to take off Mary's clothes.

"Geoff," the woman said, "come look at this, will you. Not one so bad in years. Amazing that we can keep anything at all."

The handsome man put his hands into his pockets, and clicked his tongue.

"Pretty bad, all right."

"Be still, child, stop, stop making those noises. You know perfectly well nothing is going to hurt."

"But what will you do with me?"

"That was all explained to you."

"No, no—with *me, me!*"

"You mean the cast-offs? The usual. I don't know, exactly. Somebody takes care of it."

"I want me!" Mary cried. "Not that!" She pointed at the image in the screen.

Her chair was wheeled into a semi-dark room. She was naked now, and the men lifted her to a table. The surface was like glass, black-filmed. A big machine hung above in shadows.

Straps. Clamps pulling, stretching limbs apart. The screen with the picture brought in. The men and the women, more women now. Doctor Hortel in a corner, sitting with his legs crossed, shaking his head.

Mary began to cry loudly, as hard as she could, above the hum of the mechanical things.

"Shhh. My gracious, such a racket! Just think about your job waiting for you, and all the friends you'll have and how lovely everything will be. No more troubles now."

The big machine groaned and descended from the darkness.

"Where will I find me?" Mary screamed. "What will happen to *me*?"

A long needle slid into rough flesh and the beautiful people gathered around the table.

And then they turned on the big machine.

Ray Bradbury said of Charles Beaumont (1929–1967), "Some writers are one idea people. Other writers, far rarer, far wilder, are pomegranates. They burst with seed. Chuck has always been a pomegranate writer." Charles Beaumont was a prolific and inventive writer of science fiction and horror short stories, and wrote several classic *Twillight Zone* episodes, such as "The Howling Man" and "Printer's Devil," as well as the screenplays for the films *The 7 Faces of Dr. Lao* and *The Masque of the Red Death*.

# Liking What You See: A Documentary

## Ted Chiang

If you look at the copyright page of *Uglies*, you'll see a small note at the top: "This novel was shaped by a series of e-mail exchanges between myself and Ted Chiang about his story 'Liking What You See: A Documentary.' His input on the manuscript was also invaluable."

Yes, that's all true. The story you're about to read is where the idea for the Uglies series started to bubble.

It's about a private boarding school whose approach to beauty is, in a way, the exact opposite of the Pretty system. Yes, everyone gets an operation, but not one that changes the way you look or think, but the way you *see*. No one at this school can tell whether their classmates are pretty or ugly; the part of their brain that detects human beauty has simply been switched off. So the result is the same as in *Uglies*—everyone is equal (but without the bubbleheads). Until, of course, they leave the protected environment of the school, and have to face the real world.

So here's the story that started it all. If you're an Uglies fan, don't forget that you owe some thanks to Ted, whose brilliant work is an inspiration to us all.

*Beauty is the promise of happiness.*
—STENDHAL

## Tamera Lyons, 1st-year student at Pembleton:

I can't believe it. I visited the campus last year, and I didn't hear a word about this. Now I get here and it turns out people want to make calli a requirement. One of the things I was looking forward to about college was getting rid of this, you know, so I could be like everybody else. If I'd known there was even a chance I'd have to keep it, I probably would've picked another college. I feel like I've been scammed.

I turn eighteen next week, and I'm getting my calli turned off that day. If they vote to make it a requirement, I don't know what I'll do; maybe I'll transfer, I don't know. Right now I feel like going up to people and telling them, "vote no." There's probably some campaign I can work for.

## Maria deSouza, 3rd-year student, President of the Students for Equality Everywhere (SEE):

Our goal is very simple. Pembleton University has a Code of Ethical Conduct, one that was created by the students themselves, and that all incoming students agree to follow when they enroll. The initiative that we've sponsored would add a provision to the code, requiring students to adopt calliagnosia as long as they're enrolled.

What prompted us to do this now was the release of a spex version of Visage. That's the software that, when you look at people through your spex, shows you what they'd look like with cosmetic surgery. It became a form of entertainment among a certain crowd, and a lot of college students found it offensive. When people started talking about it as a symptom of a deeper societal problem, we thought the timing was right for us to sponsor this initiative.

The deeper societal problem is lookism. For decades people've been willing to talk about racism and sexism, but they're still reluctant to talk about lookism. Yet this prejudice against unattractive people is incredibly pervasive. People do it without even being taught by anyone, which is bad enough, but instead of combating this tendency, modern society actively reinforces it.

Educating people, raising their awareness about this issue, all of that is essential, but it's not enough. That's where technology comes in. Think of calliagnosia as a kind of assisted maturity. It lets you do what you know you should: ignore the surface, so you can look deeper.

We think it's time to bring calli into the mainstream. So far the calli movement has been a minor presence on college campuses, just another one of the special-interest causes. But Pembleton isn't like other colleges, and I think the students here are ready for calli. If the initiative succeeds here, we'll be setting an example for other colleges, and ultimately, society as a whole.

## Joseph Weingartner, neurologist:

The condition is what we call an associative agnosia, rather than an apperceptive one. That means it doesn't interfere with one's visual perception, only with the ability to recognize what one sees. A calliagnosic perceives faces perfectly well; he or she can tell the difference between a pointed chin and a receding one, a straight nose and a crooked one, clear skin and blemished skin. He or she simply doesn't experience any aesthetic reaction to those differences.

Calliagnosia is possible because of the existence of certain neural pathways in the brain. All animals have criteria for evaluating the reproductive potential of prospective mates, and they've evolved neural "circuitry" to recognize those criteria. Human social interaction is centered around our faces, so our circuitry is most finely attuned to how a person's reproductive potential is manifested in his or her face. You experience the operation of that circuitry as the feeling that a person is beautiful, or ugly, or somewhere in between. By blocking the neural pathways dedicated to evaluating those features, we can induce calliagnosia.

Given how much fashions change, some people find it hard to imagine that there are absolute markers of a beautiful face. But it turns out that when people of different cultures are asked to rank photos of faces for attractiveness, some very clear patterns emerge across the board. Even very young infants show the same preference for certain faces. This lets us identify the traits that are common to everyone's idea of a beautiful face.

Probably the most obvious one is clear skin. It's the equivalent of a bright plumage in birds or a shiny coat of fur in mammals. Good skin is the single best indicator of youth and health, and it's valued in every culture. Acne may not be serious, but it *looks* like more serious diseases, and that's why we find it disagreeable.

Another trait is symmetry; we may not be conscious of millimeter differences between someone's left and right sides, but measurements reveal that individuals rated as most attractive are also the most symmetrical. And while symmetry is what our genes always aim for, it's very difficult to achieve in developmental terms; any environmental stressor—like poor nutrition, disease, parasites—tends to result in asymmetry during growth. Symmetry implies resistance to such stressors.

Other traits have to do with facial proportions. We tend to be attracted to facial proportions that are close to the population mean. That obviously depends on the population you're part of, but being near the mean usually indicates genetic health. The only departures from the mean that people consistently find attractive are ones caused by sex hormones, which suggest good reproductive potential.

Basically, calliagnosia is a lack of response to these traits; nothing more. Calliagnosics are *not* blind to fashion or cultural standards of beauty. If black lipstick is all the rage, calliagnosia won't make you forget it, although you might not notice the difference between pretty faces and plain faces wearing that lipstick. And if everyone around you sneers at people with broad noses, you'll pick up on that.

So calliagnosia by itself can't eliminate appearance-based discrimination. What it does, in a sense, is even up the odds; it takes away the innate predisposition, the tendency for such discrimination to arise in the first place. That way, if you want to teach people to ignore appearances, you won't be facing an uphill battle. Ideally you'd start with an environment where everyone's adopted calliagnosia, and then socialize them to not value appearances.

## Tamera Lyons:

People here have been asking me what it was like going to Saybrook, growing up with calli. To be honest, it's not a big deal when you're young; you know, like they say, whatever you grew up with seems normal to you. We knew that there was something that other people could see that we couldn't, but it was just something we were curious about.

For instance, my friends and I used to watch movies and try to figure out who was really good-looking and who wasn't. We'd say we could tell, but we couldn't really, not by looking at their faces. We were just going by who was the main character and who was the friend; you always knew the main character was better-looking than the friend. It's not true a hundred percent of the time, but you could usually tell if you were watching the kind of thing where the main character wouldn't be good-looking.

It's when you get older that it starts to bother you. If you hang out with people from other schools, you can feel weird because you have calli and they don't. It's not that anyone makes a big deal out of it, but it reminds you that there's something you can't see. And then you start having fights with your parents, because they're keeping you from seeing the real world. You never get anywhere with them, though.

## Richard Hamill, founder of the Saybrook School:

Saybrook came about as an outgrowth of our housing cooperative. We had maybe two dozen families at the time, all trying to establish a community based on shared values. We were holding a meeting about the possibility of starting an alternative school for our kids, and one parent mentioned the problem of the media's influence on the children. Everyone's teens were asking for cosmetic surgery so they could look like fashion models. The parents were doing their best, but you can't isolate your kids from the world; they live in an image-obsessed culture.

It was around then that the last legal challenges to calliagnosia were resolved, and we got to talking about it. We saw calli as an opportunity: What if we could live in an environment where people didn't judge each other on their appearance? What if we could raise our children in such an environment?

The school started out being just for the children of the families in the cooperative, but other calliagnosia schools began making the news, and before long people were asking if they could enroll their kids without joining the housing co-op. Eventually we set up Saybrook as a private school separate from the co-op, and one of its requirements was that parents adopt calliagnosia for as long as their kids were enrolled. Now a calliagnosia community has sprung up here, all because of the school.

## Rachel Lyons:

Tamera's father and I gave the issue a lot of thought before we decided to enroll her there. We talked to people in the community, found we liked their approach to education, but really it was visiting the school that sold me.

Saybrook has a higher than normal number of students with facial abnormalities, like bone cancer, burns, congenital conditions. Their parents moved here to keep them from being ostracized by other kids, and it works. I remember when I first visited, I saw a class of twelve-year-olds voting for class president, and they elected this girl who had burn scars on one side of her face. She was wonderfully at ease with herself, she was popular among kids who probably would have ostracized her in any other school. And I thought, this is the kind of environment I want my daughter to grow up in.

Girls have always been told that their value is tied to their appearance; their accomplishments are always magnified if they're pretty and diminished if they're not. Even worse, some girls get the message that they can get through life relying on just their looks, and then they never develop their minds. I wanted to keep Tamera away from that sort of influence.

Being pretty is fundamentally a passive quality; even when you work at it, you're working at being passive. I wanted Tamera to value herself in terms of what she could *do*, both with her mind and with her body, not in terms of how decorative she was. I didn't want her to be passive, and I'm pleased to say that she hasn't turned out that way.

## Martin Lyons:

I don't mind if Tamera decides as an adult to get rid of calli. This was never about taking choices away from her. But there's more than enough stress involved in simply getting through adolescence; the peer pressure can crush you like a paper cup. Becoming preoccupied with how you look is just one more way to be crushed, and anything that can relieve that pressure is a good thing, in my opinion.

Once you're older, you're better equipped to deal with the issue of personal appearance. You're more comfortable in your own skin, more confident, more secure. You're more likely to be satisfied with how you look, whether you're "good looking" or not. Of course not everyone reaches that level of maturity at the same age. Some people are there at sixteen, some don't get there until they're thirty or even older. But eighteen's the age of legal majority, when everyone's got the right to make their own decisions, and all you can do is trust your child and hope for the best.

## Tamera Lyons:

It'd been kind of an odd day for me. Good, but odd. I just got my calli turned off this morning.

Getting it turned off was easy. The nurse stuck some sensors on me and made me put on this helmet, and she showed me a bunch of pictures of people's faces. Then she tapped at her keyboard for a minute, and said, "I've switched off the calli," just like that. I thought you might feel something when it happened, but you don't. Then she showed me the pictures again, to make sure it worked.

When I looked at the faces again, some of them seemed . . . different. Like they were glowing, or more vivid or something. It's hard to describe. The nurse showed me my test results afterwards, and there were readings for how wide my pupils were dilating and how well my skin conducted electricity and stuff like that. And for the faces that seemed different, the readings went way up. She said those were the beautiful faces.

She said that I'd notice how other people's faces look right away, but it'd take a while before I had any reaction to how I looked. Supposedly you're too used to your face to tell.

And yeah, when I first looked in a mirror, I thought I looked totally the same. Since I got back from the doctor's, the people I see on campus definitely look different, but I still haven't noticed any difference in how I look. I've been looking at mirrors all day. For a while I was afraid that I was ugly, and any minute the ugliness was going to appear, like a rash or something. And so I've been staring at the mirror, just waiting, and nothing's happened. So I figure I'm probably not really ugly, or I'd have noticed it, but that means I'm not really pretty either, because I'd have noticed that too. So I guess that means I'm absolutely plain, you know? Exactly average. I guess that's okay.

## Joseph Weingartner:

Inducing an agnosia means simulating a specific brain lesion. We do this with a programmable pharmaceutical called neurostat; you can think of it as a highly selective anesthetic, one whose activation and targeting are all under dynamic control. We activate or deactivate the neurostat by transmitting signals through a helmet the patient puts on. The helmet also provides somatic positioning information so the neurostat molecules can triangulate their location. This lets us activate only the neurostat in a specific section of brain tissue, and keep the nerve impulses there below a specified threshold.

Neurostat was originally developed for controlling seizures in epileptics and for relief of chronic pain; it lets us treat even severe cases of these conditions without the side-effects caused by drugs that affect the entire nervous system. Later on, different neurostat protocols were developed as treatments for obsessive-compulsive disorder, addictive behavior, and various other disorders. At the same time, neurostat became incredibly valuable as a research tool for studying brain physiology.

One way neurologists have traditionally studied specialization of brain function is to observe the deficits that result from various lesions. Obviously, this technique is limited because the lesions caused by injury or disease often affect multiple functional areas. By contrast, neurostat can be activated in the tiniest portion of the brain, in effect simulating a lesion so localized that it would never occur naturally. And when you deactivate the neurostat, the "lesion" disappears and brain function returns to normal.

In this way neurologists were able to induce a wide variety of agnosias. The one most relevant here is prosopagnosia, the inability to recognize people by their faces. A prosopagnosic can't recognize friends or family members unless they say something; he can't even identify his own face in a photograph. It's not a cognitive or perceptual problem; prosopagnosics can identify people by their hairstyle, clothing, perfume, even the way they walk. The deficit is restricted purely to faces.

Prosopagnosia has always been the most dramatic indication that our brains have a special "circuit" devoted to the visual processing of faces; we look at faces in a different way than we look at anything else. And recognizing someone's face is just one of the face-processing tasks we do; there are also related circuits devoted to identifying facial expressions, and even detecting changes in the direction of another person's gaze.

One of the interesting things about prosopagnosics is that while they can't recognize a face, they still have an opinion as to whether it's attractive or not. When asked to sort photos of faces in order of attractiveness, prosopagnosics sorted the photos in pretty much the same way as anyone else. Experiments using neurostat allowed researchers to identify the neurological circuit responsible for perceiving beauty in faces, and thus essentially invent calliagnosia.

## Maria deSouza:

SEE has had extra neurostat programming helmets set up in the Student Health Office, and made arrangements so they can offer calliagnosia to anyone who wants it. You don't even have to make an appointment, you can just walk in. We're encouraging all the students to try it, at least for a day, to see what it's like. At first it seems a little odd, not seeing anyone as either good-looking or ugly, but over time you realize how positively it affects your interactions with other people.

A lot of people worry that calli might make them asexual or something, but actually physical beauty is only a small part of what makes a person attractive. No matter what a person looks like, it's much more important how the person acts; what he says and how he says it, his behavior and body language. And how does he react to you? For me, one of the things that attracts me to a guy is if *he* seems interested in *me*. It's like a feedback loop; you notice him looking at you, then he sees you looking at him, and things snowball from there. Calli doesn't change that. Plus there's that whole pheromone chemistry going on too; obviously calli doesn't affect that.

Another worry that people have is that calli will make everyone's face look the same, but that's not true either. A person's face always reflects their personality, and if anything, calli makes that clearer. You know that saying, that after a certain age, you're responsible for your face? With calli, you really appreciate how true that is. Some faces just look really bland, especially young, conventionally pretty ones. Without their physical beauty, those faces are just boring. But faces that are full of personality look as good as they ever did, maybe even better. It's like you're seeing something more essential about them.

Some people also ask about enforcement. We don't plan on doing anything like that. It's true, there's software that's pretty good at guessing if a person has calli or not, by analyzing eye-gaze patterns. But it requires a lot of data, and the campus security cams don't zoom in close enough. Everyone would have to wear personal cams, and share the data. It's possible, but that's not what we're after. We think that once people try calli, they'll see the benefits themselves.

## Tamera Lyons:

Check it out, I'm pretty!

What a day. When I woke up this morning I immediately went to the mirror; it was like I was a little kid on Christmas or something. But still, nothing; my face still looked plain. Later on I even (*laughs*) I tried to catch myself by surprise, by sneaking up on a mirror, but that didn't work. So I was kind of disappointed, and feeling just, you know, resigned to my fate.

But then this afternoon, I went out with my roommate Ina and a couple other girls from the dorm. I hadn't told anyone that I'd gotten my calli turned off, because I wanted to get used to it first. So we went to this snack bar on the other side of campus, one I hadn't been to before. We were sitting at this table, talking, and I was looking around, just seeing what people looked like without calli. And I saw this girl looking at me, and I thought, "She's really pretty." And then, (*laughs*) this'll sound really stupid, then I realized that this wall in the snack bar was a mirror, and I was looking at myself!

I can't describe it, I felt this incredible sense of *relief.* I just couldn't stop smiling! Ina asked me what I was so happy about, and I just shook my head. I went to the bathroom so I could stare at myself in the mirror for a bit.

So it's been a good day. I really *like* the way I look! It's been a good day.

## From a student debate held at Pembleton:
## Jeff Winthrop, 3rd-year student:

Of course it's wrong to judge people by their appearance, but this "blindness" isn't the answer. Education is.

Calli takes away the good as well as the bad. It doesn't just work when there's a possibility of discrimination, it keeps you from recognizing beauty altogether. There are plenty of times when looking at an attractive face doesn't hurt anyone. Calli won't let you make those distinctions, but education will.

And I know someone will say, what about when the technology gets better? Maybe one day they'll be able to insert an expert system into your brain, one that goes, "Is this an appropriate situation to apprehend beauty? If so, enjoy it; else, ignore it." Would that be okay? Would that be the "assisted maturity" you hear people talking about?

No, it wouldn't. That wouldn't be maturity; it'd be letting an expert system make your decisions for you. Maturity means seeing the differences, but realizing they don't matter. There's no technological shortcut.

## Adesh Singh, 3rd-year student:

No one's talking about letting an expert system make your decisions. What makes calli ideal is precisely that it's such a minimal change. Calli doesn't decide for you; it doesn't prevent you from doing anything. And as for maturity, you demonstrate maturity by choosing calli in the first place.

Everyone knows physical beauty has nothing to do with merit; that's what education's accomplished. But even with the best intentions in the world, people haven't stopped practicing lookism. We try to be impartial, we try not to let a person's appearance affect us, but we can't suppress our autonomic responses, and anyone who claims they can is engaged in wishful thinking. Ask yourself: don't you react differently when you meet an attractive person and when you meet an unattractive one?

Every study on this issue turns up the same results: looks help people get ahead. We can't help but think of good-looking people as more competent, more honest, more deserving than others. None of it's true, but their looks still give us that impression.

Calli doesn't blind you to anything; beauty is what blinds you. Calli lets you see.

## Tamera Lyons:

So, I've been looking at good-looking guys around campus. It's fun; weird, but fun. Like, I was in the cafeteria the other day, and I saw this guy a couple tables away, I didn't know his name, but I kept turning to look at him. I can't describe anything specific about his face, but it just seemed much more noticeable than other people's. It was like his face was a magnet, and my eyes were compass needles being pulled toward it.

And after I looked at him for a while, I found it really easy to imagine that he was a nice guy! I didn't know anything about him, I couldn't even hear what he was talking about, but I wanted to get to know him. It was kind of odd, but definitely not in a bad way.

## From a netcast of EduNews, on the American College Network:

In the latest on the Pembleton University calliagnosia initiative: EduNews has received evidence that the public-relations firm of Wyatt/Hayes paid four Pembleton students to dissuade classmates from voting for the initiative, without having them register their affiliations. Evidence includes an internal memo from Wyatt/Hayes, proposing that "good-looking students with high reputation ratings" be sought, and records of payments from the agency to Pembleton students.

The files were sent by the SemioTech Warriors, a culture-jamming group responsible for numerous acts of media vandalism.

When contacted about this story, Wyatt/Hayes issued a statement decrying this violation of their internal computer systems.

## Jeff Winthrop:

Yes, it's true, Wyatt/Hayes paid me, but it wasn't an endorsement deal; they never told me *what* to say. They just made it possible for me to devote more time to the anti-calli campaign, which is what I would've done anyway if I hadn't needed to make money tutoring. All I've been doing is expressing my honest opinion: I think calli's a bad idea.

A couple of people in the anti-calli campaign have asked that I not speak publicly about the issue anymore, because they think it would hurt the cause. I'm sorry they feel that way, because this is just an *ad hominem* attack. If you thought my arguments made sense before, this shouldn't change anything. But I realize that some people can't make those distinctions, and I'll do what's best for the cause.

## Maria deSouza:

Those students really should have registered their affiliations; we all know people who are walking endorsements. But now, whenever someone criticizes the initiative, people ask them if they're being paid. The backlash is definitely hurting the anti-calli campaign.

I consider it a compliment that someone is taking enough interest in the initiative to hire a PR firm. We've always hoped that its passing might influence people at other schools, and this means that corporations are thinking the same thing.

We've invited the president of the National Calliagnosia Association to speak on campus. Before we weren't sure if we wanted to bring the national group in, because they have a different emphasis than we do; they're more focused on the media uses of beauty, while here at SEE we're more interested in the social equality issue. But given the way students reacted to what Wyatt/Hayes did, it's clear that the media manipulation issue has the power to get us where we need to go. Our best shot at getting the initiative passed is to take advantage of the anger against advertisers. The social equality will follow afterwards.

## From the speech given at Pembleton by Walter Lambert, president of the National Calliagnosia Association:

Think of cocaine. In its natural form, as coca leaves, it's appealing, but not to an extent that it usually becomes a problem. But refine it, purify it, and you get a compound that hits your pleasure receptors with an unnatural intensity. That's when it becomes addictive.

Beauty has undergone a similar process, thanks to advertisers. Evolution gave us a circuit that responds to good looks—call it the pleasure receptor for our visual cortex—and in our natural environment, it was useful to have. But take a person with one-in-a-million skin and bone structure, add professional makeup and retouching, and you're no longer looking at beauty in its natural form. You've got pharmaceutical-grade beauty, the cocaine of good looks.

Biologists call this "supernormal stimulus"; show a mother bird a giant plastic egg, and she'll incubate it instead of her own real eggs. Madison Avenue has saturated our environment with this kind of stimuli, this visual drug. Our beauty receptors receive more stimulation than they were evolved to handle; we're seeing more beauty in one day than our ancestors did in a lifetime. And the result is that beauty is slowly ruining our lives.

How? The way any drug becomes a problem: by interfering with our relationships with other people. We become dissatisfied with the way ordinary people look because they can't compare to supermodels. Two-dimensional images are bad enough, but now with spex, advertisers can put a supermodel right in front of you, making eye contact. Software companies offer goddesses who'll remind you of your appointments. We've all heard about men who prefer virtual girlfriends over actual ones, but they're not the only ones who've been affected. The more time any of us spend with gorgeous digital apparitions around, the more our relationships with real human beings are going to suffer.

We can't avoid these images and still live in the modern world. And that means we can't kick this habit, because beauty is a drug you can't abstain from unless you literally keep your eyes closed all the time.

Until now. Now you can get another set of eyelids, one that blocks out this drug, but still lets you see. And that's calliagnosia. Some people call it excessive, but I call it just enough. Technology is being used to manipulate us through our emotional reactions, so it's only fair that we use it to protect ourselves too.

Right now you have an opportunity to make an enormous impact. The Pembleton student body has always been at the vanguard of every progressive movement; what you decide here will set an example for students across the country. By passing this initiative, by adopting calliagnosia, you'll be sending a message to advertisers that young people are no longer willing to be manipulated.

## From a netcast of EduNews:

Following NCA president Walter Lambert's speech, polls show that 54% of the Pembleton University students support the calliagnosia initiative. Polls across the country show that an average of 28% of students would support a similar initiative at their school, an increase of 8% in the past month.

## Tamera Lyons:

I thought he went overboard with that cocaine analogy. Do you know anyone who steals stuff and sells it so he can get his fix of advertising?

But I guess he has a point about how good-looking people are in commercials versus in real life. It's not that they look better than people in real life, but they look good in a different way.

Like, I was at the campus store the other today, and I needed to check my e-mail, and when I put on my spex I saw this poster running a commercial. It was for some shampoo, Jouissance I think. I'd seen it before, but it was different without calli. The model was so—I couldn't take my eyes off her. I don't mean I felt the same as that time I saw the good-looking guy in the cafeteria; it wasn't like I wanted to get to know her. It was more like . . . watching a sunset, or a fireworks display.

I just stood there and watched the commercial like five times, just so I could look at her some more. I didn't think a human being could look so, you know, spectacular.

But it's not like I'm going to quit talking to people so I can watch commercials through my spex all the time. Watching them is very intense, but it's a totally different experience than looking at a real person. And it's not even like I immediately want to go out and buy everything they're selling, either. I'm not even really paying attention to the products. I just think they're amazing to watch.

## Maria deSouza:

If I'd met Tamera earlier, I might have tried to persuade her not to get her calli turned off. I doubt I would've succeeded; she seems pretty firm about her decision. Even so, she's a great example of the benefits of calli. You can't help but notice it when you talk to her. For example, at one point I was saying how lucky she was, and she said, "Because I'm beautiful?" And she was being totally sincere! Like she was talking about her height. Can you imagine a woman without calli saying that?

Tamera is completely unself-conscious about her looks; she's not vain or insecure, and she can describe herself as beautiful without embarrassment. I gather that she's very pretty, and with a lot of women who look like that, I can see something in their manner, a hint of showoffishness. Tamera doesn't have that. Or else they display false modesty, which is also easy to tell, but Tamera doesn't do that either, because she truly is modest. There's no way she could be like that if she hadn't been raised with calli. I just hope she stays that way.

## Annika Lindstrom, 2nd-year student:

I think this calli thing is a terrible idea. I like it when guys notice me, and I'd be really disappointed if they stopped.

I think this whole thing is just a way for people who, honestly, aren't very good looking to try and make themselves feel better. And the only way they can do that is to punish people who have what they don't. And that's just unfair.

Who wouldn't want to be pretty if they could? Ask anyone, ask the people behind this, and I bet you they'd all say yes. Okay, sure, being pretty means that you'll be hassled by jerks sometimes. There are always jerks, but that's part of life. If those scientists could come up with some way to turn off the jerk circuit in guys' brains, I'd be all in favor of that.

## Jolene Carter, 3rd-year student:

I'm voting for the initiative, because I think it'd be a relief if everyone had calli.

People are nice to me because of how I look, and part of me likes that, but part of me feels guilty because I haven't done anything to deserve it. And sure, it's nice to have men pay attention to me, but it can be hard to make a real connection with someone. Whenever I like a guy, I always wonder how much he's interested in me, versus how much he's interested in my looks. It can be hard to tell, because all relationships are wonderful at the beginning, you know? It's not until later that you find out whether you can really be comfortable with each other. It was like that with my last boyfriend. He wasn't happy with me if I didn't look fabulous, so I was never able to truly relax. But by that time I realized that, I'd already let myself get close to him, so that really hurt, finding out that he didn't see the real me.

And then there's how you feel around other women. I don't think most women like it, but you're always comparing how you look relative to everyone else. Sometimes I feel like I'm in a competition, and I don't want to be.

I thought about getting calli once, but it didn't seem like it would help unless everyone else did too; getting it all by myself wouldn't change the way others treat me. But if everyone on campus had calli, I'd be glad to get it.


## Tamera Lyons:

I was showing my roommate Ina this album of pictures from high school, and we get to all these pictures of me and Garrett, my ex. So Ina wants to know all about him, and so I tell her. I'm telling her how we were together all of senior year, and how much I loved him, and wanted us to stay together, but he wanted to be free to date when he went to college. And then she's like, "You mean *he* broke up with *you*?"

It took me a while before I could get her to tell me what was up; she made me promise twice not to get mad. Eventually she said Garrett isn't exactly good-looking. I was thinking he must be average-looking, because he didn't really look that different after I got my calli turned off. But Ina said he was definitely below average.

She found pictures of a couple other guys who she thought looked like him, and with them I could see how they're not good-looking. Their faces just look goofy. Then I took another look at Garrett's picture, and I guess he's got some of the same features, but on him they look cute. To me, anyway.

I guess it's true what they say: love is a little bit like calli. When you love someone, you don't really see what they look like. I don't see Garrett the way others do, because I still have feelings for him.

Ina said she couldn't believe someone who looked like him would break up with someone who looked like me. She said that in a school without calli, he probably wouldn't have been able to get a date with me. Like, we wouldn't be in the same league.

That's weird to think about. When Garrett and I were going out, I always thought we were meant to be together. I don't mean that I believe in destiny, but I just thought there was something really right about the two of us. So the idea that we could've both been in the same school, but not gotten together because we didn't have calli, feels strange. And I know that Ina can't be sure of that. But I can't be sure she's wrong, either.

And maybe that means I should be glad I had calli, because it let me and Garrett get together. I don't know about that.

## From a netcast of EduNews:

Netsites for a dozen calliagnosia student organizations around the country were brought down today in a coordinated denial-of-service attack. Although no one has claimed credit for the attack, it's been suggested that those responsible may be retaliating for an incident last month in which the American Association of Cosmetic Surgeons' netsite was replaced by a calliagnosia site.

In a related story, the SemioTech Warriors announced the release of their new "Dermatology" computer virus. This virus has quickly begun infecting video servers around the world, altering netcasts so that faces and bodies exhibit conditions such as acne and varicose veins.

## Warren Davidson, 1st-year student:

I thought about trying calli before, when I was in high school, but I never knew how to bring it up with my parents. So when they started offering it here, I figured I'd give it a try. (*shrugs*) It's okay.

Actually, it's better than okay. (*pause*) I've always hated how I look. For a while in high school I couldn't stand the sight of myself in a mirror. But with calli, I don't mind as much. I know I look the same to other people, but that doesn't seem as big a deal as it used to. I feel better just by not being reminded that some people are so much better-looking than others. Like, for instance: I was helping this girl in the library with a problem on her calculus homework, and afterwards I realized that she's someone I'd thought was really pretty. Normally I would have been really nervous around her, but with calli, she wasn't so hard to talk to.

Maybe she thinks I look like a freak, I don't know, but the thing was, when I was talking to her *I* didn't think I looked like a freak. Before I got calli, I think I was just too self-conscious, and that just made things worse. Now I'm more relaxed.

It's not like I suddenly feel all wonderful about myself or anything, and I'm sure for other people calli wouldn't help them at all, but for me, calli makes me not feel as bad as I used to. And that's worth something.

## Alex Bibescu, professor of religious studies at Pembleton:

Some people have been quick to dismiss the whole calliagnosia debate as superficial, an argument over makeup or who can and can't get a date. But if you actually look at it, you'll see it's much deeper than that. It reflects a very old ambivalence about the body, one that's been part of Western civilization since ancient times.

You see, the foundations of our culture were laid in classical Greece, where physical beauty and the body were celebrated. But our culture is also thoroughly permeated by the monotheistic tradition, which devalues the body in favor of the soul. These old conflicting impulses are rearing their heads again, this time in the calliagnosia debate.

I suspect that most calli supporters think of themselves to be modern, secular liberals, and wouldn't admit to being influenced by monotheism in any way. But take a look at who else advocates calliagnosia: conservative religious groups. There are communities of all three major monotheistic faiths—Jewish, Christian, and Muslim—who've begun using calli to make their young members more resistant to the charms of outsiders. This commonality is no coincidence. The liberal calli supporters may not use language like "resisting the temptations of the flesh," but in their own way, they're following the same tradition of deprecating the physical.

Really, the only calli supporters who can credibly claim they're not influenced by monotheism are the NeoMind Buddhists. They're a sect who see calliagnosia as a step toward enlightened thought, because it eliminates one's perception of illusory distinctions. But the NeoMind sect is open to broad use of neurostat as an aid to meditation, which is a radical stance of an entirely different sort. I doubt you'll find many modern liberals or conservative monotheists sympathetic to that!

So you see, this debate isn't just about commercials and cosmetics, it's about determining what's the appropriate relationship between the mind and the body. Are we more fully realized when we minimize the physical part of our natures? And that, you have to agree, is a profound question.

## Joseph Weingartner:

After calliagnosia was discovered, some researchers wondered if it might be possible to create an analogous condition that rendered the subject blind to race or ethnicity. They've made a number of attempts—impairing various levels of category discrimination in tandem with face recognition, that sort of thing—but the resulting deficits were always unsatisfactory. Usually the test subjects would simply be unable to distinguish similar-looking individuals. One test actually produced a benign variant of Fregoli syndrome, causing the subject to mistake every person he met for a family member. Unfortunately, treating everyone like a brother isn't desirable in so literal a sense.

When neurostat treatments for problems like compulsive behavior entered widespread use, a lot of people thought that "mind programming" was finally here. People asked their doctors if they could get the same sexual tastes as their spouses. Media pundits worried about the possibility of programming loyalty to a government or corporation, or belief in an ideology or religion.

The fact is, we have no access to the contents of anyone's thoughts. We can shape broad aspects of personality, we can make changes consistent with the natural specialization of the brain, but these are extremely coarse-grained adjustments. There's no neural pathway that specifically handles resentment toward immigrants, any more than there's one for Marxist doctrine or foot fetishism. If we ever get true mind programming, we'll be able to create "race blindness," but until then, education is our best hope.

## Tamera Lyons:

I had an interesting class today. In History of Ideas, we've got this T.A., he's named Anton, and he was saying how a lot of words we use to describe an attractive person used to be words for magic. Like the word "charm" originally meant a magic spell, and the word "glamour" did, too. And it's just blatant with words like "enchanting" and "spellbinding." And when he said that, I thought, yeah, that's what it's like: seeing a really good-looking person is like having a magic spell cast over you.

And Anton was saying how one of the primary uses of magic was to create love and desire in someone. And that makes total sense, too, when you think about those words "charm" and "glamour." Because seeing beauty feels like love. You feel like you've got a crush on a really good-looking person, just by looking at them.

And I've been thinking that maybe there's a way I can get back together with Garrett. Because if Garrett didn't have calli, maybe he'd fall in love with me again. Remember how I said before that maybe calli was what let us get together? Well, maybe calli is actually what's keeping us apart now. Maybe Garrett would want to get back with me if he saw what I really looked like.

Garrett turned eighteen during the summer, but he never got his calli turned off because he didn't think it was a big deal. He goes to Northrop now. So I called him up, just as a friend, and when we were talking about stuff, I asked him what he thought about the calli initiative here at Pembleton. He said he didn't see what all the fuss was about, and then I told him how much I liked not having calli anymore, and said he ought to try it, so he could judge both sides. He said that made sense. I didn't make a big deal out of it, but I was stoked.

## Daniel Taglia, professor of comparative literature at Pembleton:

The student initiative doesn't apply to faculty, but obviously if it passes there'll be pressure on the faculty to adopt calliagnosia as well. So I don't consider it premature for me to say that I'm adamantly opposed to it.

This is just the latest example of political correctness run amok. The people advocating calli are well-intentioned, but what they're doing is infantilizing us. The very notion that beauty is something we need to be protected from is insulting. Next thing you know, a student organization will insist we all adopt music agnosia, so we don't feel bad about ourselves when we hear gifted singers or musicians.

When you watch Olympic athletes in competition, does your self-esteem plummet? Of course not. On the contrary, you feel wonder and admiration; you're inspired that such exceptional individuals exist. So why can't we feel the same way about beauty? Feminism would have us apologize for having that reaction. It wants to replace aesthetics with politics, and to the extent it's succeeded, it's impoverished us.

Being in the presence of a world-class beauty can be as thrilling as listening to a world-class soprano. Gifted individuals aren't the only ones who benefit from their gifts; we *all* do. Or, I should say, we all *can*. Depriving ourselves of that opportunity would be a crime.

## Commercial paid for by People for Ethical Nanomedicine:

*Voiceover:*
Have your friends been telling you that calli is cool, that it's the smart thing to do? Then maybe you should talk to people who grew up with calli.

"After I got my calli turned off, I recoiled the first time I met an unattractive person. I knew it was silly, but I just couldn't help myself. Calli didn't help make me mature, it *kept* me from becoming mature. I had to relearn how to interact with people."

"I went to school to be a graphic artist. I worked day and night, but I never got anywhere with it. My teacher said I didn't have the eye for it, that calli had stunted me aesthetically. There's no way I can get back what I've lost."

"Having calli was like having my parents inside my head, censoring my thoughts. Now that I've had it turned off, I realize just what kind of abuse I'd been living with."

*Voiceover:*

If the people who grew up with calliagnosia don't recommend it, shouldn't that tell you something?

They didn't have a choice, but you do. Brain damage is never a good idea, no matter what your friends say.

## Maria deSouza:

We'd never heard of the People for Ethical Nanomedicine, so we did some research on them. It took some digging, but it turns out it's not a grassroots organization at all, it's an industry PR front. A bunch of cosmetics companies got together recently and created it. We haven't been able to contact the people who appear in the commercial, so we don't know how much, if any, of what they said was true. Even if they were being honest, they certainly aren't typical; most people who get their calli turned off feel fine about it. And there are definitely graphic artists who grew up with calli.

It kind of reminds me of an ad I saw a while back, put out by a modeling agency when the calli movement was just getting started. It was just a picture of a supermodel's face, with a caption: "If you no

longer saw her as beautiful, whose loss would it be? Hers, or yours?"
This new campaign has the same message, basically saying, "You'll
be sorry," but instead of taking that cocky attitude, it has more of
a concerned-warning tone. This is classic PR: hide behind a nice-
sounding name, and create the impression of a third party looking
out for the consumer's interests.

## Tamera Lyons:

I thought that commercial was totally idiotic. It's not like I'm in
favor of the initiative—I don't want people to vote for it—but people shouldn't vote against it for the wrong reason. Growing up with
calli isn't crippling. There's no reason for anyone to feel sorry for
me or anything. I'm dealing with it fine. And that's why I think
people ought to vote against the initiative: because seeing beauty
is fine.

Anyway, I talked to Garrett again. He said he'd just gotten his
calli turned off. He said it seemed cool so far, although it was kind of
weird, and I told him I felt the same way when I got mine disabled.
I suppose it's kind of funny, how I was acting like an old pro, even
though I've only had mine off for a few weeks.

## Joseph Weingartner:

One of the first questions researchers asked about calliagnosia was
whether it has any "spillover," that is, whether it affects your appreci-
ation of beauty outside of faces. For the most part, the answer seems
to be "no." Calliagnosics seem to enjoy looking at the same things
other people do. That said, we can't rule out the possibility of side
effects.

As an example, consider the spillover that's observed in prosopagnosics. One prosopagnosic who was a dairy farmer found he

could no longer recognize his cows individually. Another found it harder to distinguish models of cars, if you can imagine that. These cases suggest that we sometimes use our face-recognition module for tasks other than strict face recognition. We may not think something looks like a face—a car, for example—but at a neurological level we're treating it as if it were a face.

There may be a similar spillover among calliagnosics, but since calliagnosia is subtler than prosopagnosia, any spillover is harder to measure. The role of fashion in cars' appearances, for example, is vastly greater than its role in faces', and there's little consensus about which cars are most attractive. There may be a calliagnosic out there who doesn't enjoy looking at certain models as much as he otherwise would, but he hasn't come forward to complain.

Then there's the role our beauty-recognition module plays in our aesthetic reaction to symmetry. We appreciate symmetry in a wide range of settings—painting, sculpture, graphic design—but at the same time we also appreciate asymmetry. There are a lot of factors that contribute to our reaction to art, and not much consensus about when a particular example is successful.

It might be interesting to see if calliagnosia communities produce fewer truly talented visual artists, but given how few such individuals arise in the general population, it's difficult to do a statistically meaningful study. The only thing we know for certain is that calliagnosics report a more muted response to some portraits, but that's not a side effect *per se*; portrait paintings derive at least some of their impact from the facial appearance of the subject.

Of course, any effect is too much for some people. This is the reason given by some parents for not wanting calliagnosia for their children: they want their children to be able to appreciate the Mona Lisa, and perhaps create its successor.

## Marc Esposito, 4th-year student at Waterston College:

That Pembleton thing sounds totally crazed. I could see doing it like a setup for some prank. You know, as in, you'd fix this guy up with a girl, and tell him she's an absolute babe, but actually you've fixed him up with a dog, and he can't tell so he believes you. That'd be kind of funny, actually.

But I sure as hell would never get this calli thing. I want to date good-looking girls. Why would I want something that'd make me lower my standards? Okay, sure, some nights all the babes have been taken, and you have to choose from the leftovers. But that's why there's beer, right? Doesn't mean I want to wear beer goggles all the time.

## Tamera Lyons:

So Garrett and I were talking on the phone again last night, and I asked him if he wanted to switch to video so we could see each other. And he said okay, so we did.

I was casual about it, but I had actually spent a lot of time getting ready. Ina's teaching me to put on makeup, but I'm not very good at it yet, I got that phone software that makes it look like you're wearing makeup. I set it for just a little bit, and I think it made a real difference in how I looked. Maybe it was overkill, I don't know how much Garrett could tell, but I just wanted to be sure I looked as good as possible.

As soon as we switched to video, I could see him react. It was like his eyes got wider. He was like, "You look really great," and I was like, "Thanks." Then he got shy, and made some joke about the way he looked, but I told him I liked the way he looked.

We talked for a while on video, and all the time I was really conscious of him looking at me. That felt good. I got a feeling that he was thinking he might want us to get back together again, but maybe I was just imagining it.

Maybe next time we talk I'll suggest he could come visit me for a weekend, or I could go visit him at Northrop. That'd be really cool. Though I'd have to be sure I could do my own makeup before that.

I know there's no guarantee that he'll want to get back together. Getting my calli turned off didn't make me love him less, so maybe it won't make him love me any more. I'm hoping, though.

## Cathy Minami, 3rd-year student:

Anyone who says the calli movement is good for women is spreading the propaganda of all oppressors: the claim that subjugation is actually protection. Calli supporters want to demonize those women who possess beauty. Beauty can provide just as much pleasure for those who have it as for those who perceive it, but the calli movement makes women feel guilty about taking pleasure in their appearance. It's yet another patriarchal strategy for suppressing female sexuality, and once again, too many women have bought into it.

Of *course* beauty has been used as a tool of oppression, but eliminating beauty is not the answer; you can't liberate people by narrowing the scope of their experiences. That's positively Orwellian. What's needed is a woman-centered concept of beauty, one that lets all women feel good about themselves instead of making most of them feel bad.

## Lawrence Sutton, 4th-year student:

I totally knew what Walter Lambert was talking about in his speech. I wouldn't have phrased it the way he did, but I've felt the same way for a while now. I got calli a couple years ago, long before this initiative came up, because I wanted to be able to concentrate on more important things.

I don't mean I only think about schoolwork; I've got a girlfriend, and we have a good relationship. That hasn't changed. What's changed is how I interact with advertising. Before, every time I used to walk past a magazine stand or see a commercial, I could feel my attention being drawn a little bit. It was like they were trying to arouse me against my will. I don't necessarily mean a sexual kind of arousal, but they were trying to appeal to me on a visceral level. And I would automatically resist, and go back to whatever I was doing before. But it was a distraction, and resisting those distractions took energy that I could have been using elsewhere.

But now with calli, I don't feel that pull. Calli freed me from that distraction, it gave me that energy back. So I'm totally in favor of it.

## Lori Harber, 3rd-year student at Maxwell College:

Calli is for wusses. My attitude is, fight back. Go radical ugly. That's what the beautiful people need to see.

I got my nose taken off about this time last year. It's a bigger deal than it sounds, surgery-wise; to be healthy and stuff, you have to move some of the hairs further in to catch dust. And the bone you see (*taps it with a fingernail*) isn't real, it's ceramic. Having your real bone exposed is a big infection risk.

I like it when I freak people out; sometimes I actually ruin some-one's appetite when they're eating. But freaking people out, that's not what it's *about*. It's about how ugly can beat beautiful at its own game. I get more looks walking down the street than a beautiful woman. You see me standing next to a video model, who you going to notice more? Me, that's who. You won't want to, but you will.

## Tamera Lyons:

Garrett and I were talking again last night, and we got to talking about, you know, if either of us had been going out with someone else. And I was casual about it, I said that had hung out with some guys, but nothing major.

So I asked him the same. He was kind of embarrassed about it, but eventually he said that he was finding it harder to, like, really become friendly with girls in college, harder than he expected. And now he's thinking it's because of the way he looks.

I just said, "No way," but I didn't really know what to say. Part of me was glad that Garrett isn't seeing someone else yet, and part of me felt bad for him, and part of me was just surprised. I mean, he's smart, he's funny, he's a great guy, and I'm not just saying that because I went out with him. He was popular in high school.

But then I remembered what Ina said about me and Garrett. I guess being smart and funny doesn't mean you're in the same league as someone, you have to be equally good-looking too. And if Garrett's been talking to girls who are pretty, maybe they don't feel like he's in their league.

I didn't make a big deal out of it when we were talking, because I don't think he wanted to talk about it a lot. But afterwards, I was thinking that if we decide to do a visit, I should definitely go out to Northrop to see him instead of him coming here. Obviously, I'm hoping something'll happen between us, but also, I thought, maybe if the other people at his school see us together, he might feel better. Because I know sometimes that works: if you're hanging out with a cool person, you feel cool, and other people think you're cool. Not that I'm super cool, but I guess people like how I look, so I thought it might help.

## Ellen Hutchinson, professor of sociology at Pembleton:

I admire the students who are putting forth this initiative. Their idealism heartens me, but I have mixed feelings about their goal.

Like anyone else who's my age, I've had to come to terms with the effects time has had on my appearance. It wasn't an easy thing to get used to, but I've reached the point where I'm content with the way I look. Although I can't deny that I'm curious to see what a calli-only community would be like; maybe there a woman my age wouldn't become invisible when a young woman entered the room.

But would I have wanted to adopt calli when I was young? I don't know. I'm sure it would've spared me some of the distress I felt about growing older. But I *liked* the way I looked when I was young. I wouldn't have wanted to give that up. I'm not sure if, as I grew older, there was ever a point when the benefits would have outweighed the costs for me.

And these students, they might never even lose the beauty of youth. With the gene therapies coming out now, they'll probably look young for decades, maybe even their entire lives. They might never have to make the adjustments I did, in which case adopting calli wouldn't even save them from pain later on. So the idea that they might voluntarily give up one of the pleasures of youth is almost galling. Sometimes I want to shake them and say, "No! Don't you realize what you have?"

I've always liked young people's willingness to fight for their beliefs. That's one reason I've never really believed in the cliché that youth is wasted on the young. But this initiative would bring the cliché closer to reality, and I would hate for that to be the case.

## Joseph Weingartner:

I've tried calliagnosia for a day; I've tried a wide variety of agnosias for limited periods. Most neurologists do, so we can better understand these conditions and empathize with our patients. But I couldn't adopt calliagnosia on a long-term basis, if for no other reason than that I see patients.

There's a slight interaction between calliagnosia and the ability to gauge a person's health visually. It certainly doesn't make you blind to things like a person's skin tone, and a calliagnosic can recognize symptoms of illness just like anyone else does; this is something that general cognition handles perfectly well. But physicians need to be sensitive to very subtle cues when evaluating a patient; sometimes you use your intuition when making a diagnosis, and calliagnosia would act as a handicap in such situations.

Of course, I'd be disingenuous if I claimed that professional requirements were the only thing keeping me from adopting calliagnosia. The more relevant question is, would I choose calliagnosia if I did nothing but lab research and never dealt with patients? And to that, my answer is, no. Like many other people, I enjoy seeing a pretty face, but I consider myself mature enough to not let that affect my judgment.

## Tamera Lyons:

I can't believe it, Garrett got his calli turned back on.

We were talking on the phone last night, just ordinary stuff, and I ask him if he wants to switch to video. And he's like, "Okay," so we do. And then I realize he's not looking at me the same way he was before. So I ask him if everything's okay with him, and that's when he tells me about getting calli again.

He said he did it because he wasn't happy about the way he looked. I asked him if someone had said something about it, because he should ignore them, but he said it wasn't that. He just didn't like how he felt when he saw himself in a mirror. So I was like, "What are you talking about, you look cute." I tried to get him to give it another chance, saying stuff like, he should spend more time without calli before making any decisions. Garrett said he'd think about it, but I don't know what he's going to do.

Anyway, afterwards, I was thinking about what I'd said to him. Did I tell him that because I don't like calli, or because I wanted him to see how I looked? I mean, of course I liked the way he looked at me, and I was hoping it would lead somewhere, but it's not as if I'm being inconsistent, is it? If I'd always been in favor of calli, but made an exception when it came to Garrett, that'd be different. But I'm against calli, so it's not like that.

Oh, who am I kidding? I wanted Garrett to get his calli turned off for my own benefit, not because I'm anti-calli. And it's not even that I'm anti-calli, so much, as I am against calli being a requirement. I don't want anyone else deciding calli's right for me: not my parents, not a student organization. But if someone decides they want calli themselves, that's fine, whatever. So I should let Garrett decide for himself, I know that.

It's just frustrating. I mean, I had this whole plan figured out, with Garrett finding me irresistible, and realizing what a mistake he'd made. So I'm disappointed, that's all.

## From Maria deSouza's speech the day before the election:

We've reached a point where we can begin to adjust our minds. The question is, when is it appropriate for us to do so? We shouldn't automatically accept that natural is better, nor should we automatically presume that we can improve on nature. It's up to us to decide which qualities we value, and what's the best way to achieve those.

I say that physical beauty is something we no longer need.

Calli doesn't mean that you'll never see anyone as beautiful. When you see a smile that's genuine, you'll see beauty. When you see an act of courage or generosity, you'll see beauty. Most of all, when you look at someone you love, you'll see beauty. All calli does is keep you from being distracted by surfaces. True beauty is what you see with the eyes of love, and that's something that nothing can obscure.

## From the speech netcast by Rebecca Boyer, spokesperson for People for Ethical Nanomedicine, the day before the election:

You might be able to create a pure calli society in an artificial setting, but in the real world, you're never going to get a hundred percent compliance. And that is calli's weakness. Calli works fine if every-body has it, but if even one person doesn't, that person will take advantage of everyone else.

There'll always be people who don't get calli; you know that. Just think about what those people could do. A manager could pro-mote attractive employees and demote ugly ones, but you won't even notice. A teacher could reward attractive students and punish ugly ones, but you won't be able to tell. All the discrimination you hate could be taking place, without you even realizing.

Of course, it's possible those things won't happen. But if peo-ple could always be trusted to do what's right, no one would have suggested calli in the first place. In fact, the people prone to such behavior are liable to do it even more once there's no chance of their getting caught.

If you're outraged by that sort of lookism, how can you afford to get calli? You're precisely the type of person who's needed to blow the whistle on that behavior, but if you've got calli, you won't be able to recognize it.

If you want to fight discrimination, keep your eyes open.

## From a netcast of EduNews:

The calliagnosia initiative sponsored by students at Pembleton Uni-versity was defeated by a vote of sixty-four percent to thirty-six percent.

Polls showed a majority favoring the initiative until days before the election. Many students say they were previously planning to vote for the initiative, but reconsidered after seeing the speech given by Rebecca Boyer of the People for Ethical Nanomedicine. This despite an earlier revelation that PEN was established by cosmetics companies to oppose the calliagnosia movement.

## Maria deSouza:

Of course it's disappointing, but we originally thought of the initiative as a long shot. That period when the majority supported it was something of a fluke, so I can't be too disappointed about people changing their minds. The important thing is that people everywhere are talking about the value of appearances, and more of them are thinking about calli seriously.

And we're not stopping; in fact, the next few years will be a very exciting time. A spex manufacturer just demonstrated some new technology that could change everything. They've figured out a way to fit somatic positioning beacons in a pair of spex, custom-calibrated for a single person. That means no more helmet, no more office visit needed to reprogram your neurostat; you can just put on your spex and do it yourself. That means you'll be able to turn your calli on or off, *any time you want.*

That means we won't have the problem of people feeling that they have to give up beauty altogether. Instead, we can promote the idea that beauty is appropriate in some situations and not in others. For example, people could keep calli enabled when they're working, but disable it when they're among friends. I think people recognize that calli offers benefits, and will choose it on at least a part-time basis.

I'd say the ultimate goal is for calli to be considered the proper way to behave in polite society. People can always disable their calli in private, but the default for public interaction would be freedom from lookism. Appreciating beauty would become a consensual interaction, something you do only when both parties, the beholder and the beheld, agree to it.

## From a netcast of EduNews:

In the latest developments regarding the Pembleton calliagnosia initiative, EduNews has learned that a new form of digital manipulation was used on the netcast of PEN spokesperson Rebecca Boyer's speech. EduNews has received files from the SemioTech Warriors that contain what appear to be two recorded versions of the speech: an original, acquired from the Wyatt/Hayes computers, and the netcast version. The files also include the SemioTech Warriors' analysis of the differences between the two versions.

The discrepancies are primarily enhancements to Ms. Boyer's voice intonation, facial expressions, and body language. Viewers who watched the original version rate Ms. Boyer's performance as good, while those who watched the edited version rate her performance as excellent, describing her as extraordinarily dynamic and persuasive. Based on their analysis, the SemioTech Warriors believe that Wyatt/Hayes has developed new software capable of fine-tuning paralinguistic cues in order to maximize the emotional response evoked in viewers. This dramatically increases the effectiveness of recorded presentations, especially when viewed through spex, and its use in the PEN netcast is likely what caused many supporters of the calliagnosia initiative to change their votes.

## Walter Lambert, president of the National Calliagnosia Association:

In my entire career, I've met only a couple people who have the kind of charisma they gave Ms. Boyer in that speech. People like that radiate a kind of reality-distortion field that lets them convince you of almost anything. You feel moved by their very presence, you're ready to open your wallet or agree to whatever they ask. It's not until later that you remember all the objections you had, but by then, often as not, it's too late. And I'm truly frightened by the prospect of corporations being able to generate that effect with software.

What this is, is another kind of supernormal stimuli, like flawless beauty but even more dangerous. We had a defense against beauty, and Wyatt/Hayes has escalated things to the next level. And protecting ourselves from this type of persuasion is going to be a hell of a lot harder.

There is a type of tonal agnosia, or aprosodia, that makes you unable to hear voice intonation; all you hear are the words, not the delivery. There's also an agnosia that prevents you from recognizing facial expressions. Adopting the two of these would protect you from this type of manipulation, because you'd have to judge a speech purely on its content; its delivery would be invisible to you. But I can't recommend them. The result is nothing like calli. If you can't hear tone of voice or read someone's expression, your ability to interact with others is crippled. It'd be a kind of high-functioning autism. A few NCA members *are* adopting both agnosias, as a form of protest, but no one expects many people will follow their example.

So that means that once this software gets into widespread use, we're going to be facing extraordinarily persuasive pitches from all sides: commercials, press releases, evangelists. We'll hear the most stirring speeches given by a politician or general in decades. Even activists and culture jammers will use it, just to keep up with the establishment. Once the range of this software gets wide enough, even the movies will use it, too: an actor's own ability won't matter, because everyone's performance will be uncanny.

The same thing'll happen as happened with beauty: our environment will become saturated with this supernormal stimuli, and it'll affect our interaction with real people. When every speaker on a netcast has the presence of a Winston Churchill or a Martin Luther King, we'll begin to regard ordinary people, with their average use of paralinguistic cues, as bland and unpersuasive. We'll become dissatisfied with the people we interact with in real life, because they won't be as engaging as the projections we see through our spex.

I just hope those spex for reprogramming neurostat hit the market soon. Then maybe we can encourage people to adopt the stronger agnosias just when they're watching video. That may be the only way for us to preserve authentic human interaction: if we save our emotional responses for real life.

## Tamera Lyons:

I know how this is going to sound, but . . . well, I'm thinking about getting my calli turned back on.

In a way, it's because of that PEN video. I don't mean I'm getting calli just because makeup companies don't want people to and I'm angry at them. That's not it. But it's hard to explain.

I *am* angry at them, because they used a trick to manipulate people; they weren't playing fair. But what it made me realize was, I was doing the same kind of thing to Garrett. Or I wanted to, anyway. I was trying to use my looks to win him back. And in a way that's not playing fair, either.

I don't mean that I'm as bad as the advertisers are! I love Garrett, and they just want to make money. But remember when I was talking about beauty as a kind of magic spell? It gives you an advantage, and I think it's very easy to misuse something like that. And what calli does is make a person immune to that sort of spell. So I figure I shouldn't mind if Garrett would rather be immune, because I shouldn't be trying to gain an advantage in the first place. If I get him back, I want it to be by playing fair, by him loving me for myself.

I know, just because he got his calli turned back on doesn't mean that I have to. I've really been enjoying seeing what faces look like. But if Garrett's going to be immune, I feel like I should be too. So we're even, you know? And if we do get back together, maybe we'll get those new spex they're talking about. Then we can turn off our calli when we're by ourselves, just the two of us.

And I guess calli makes sense for other reasons, too. Those makeup companies and everyone else, they're just trying to create needs in you that you wouldn't feel if they were playing fair, and I don't like that. If I'm going to be dazzled watching a commercial, it'll be when I'm in the mood, not whenever they spring it on me. Although I'm not going to get those other agnosias, like that tonal one, not yet anyway. Maybe once those new spex come out.

This doesn't mean I agree with my parents' having me grow up with calli. I still think they were wrong; they thought getting rid of beauty would help make a utopia, and I don't believe that at all. Beauty isn't the problem, it's how some people are misusing it that's the problem. And that's what calli's good for; it lets you guard against that. I don't know, maybe this wasn't a problem back in my parents' day. But it's something we have to deal with now.

———————

Ted Chiang is the author of *Stories of Your Life and Others*, where "Liking What You See" was first published. His short fiction has won the Hugo, Nebula, Sturgeon, and Locus awards. He lives outside of Seattle, Washington.

# Naturally Unnatural

## The Postnatural Politics of the Uglies *Series*

### Will Shetterly

So what does it mean to be human?

In Tally's world, it can mean radical cosmetic surgery, eyescreens, skintennas, amped-up muscles, calorie purgers, manga eyes, cutting, and even intentional brain damage. But that's all future stuff, right? Most normal, present-day people would never do things that are so . . . unnatural. And people in the olden days were even less freaky than us, right?

Will Shetterly would respectfully disagree. In this essay, he explains how much of human history is more like Tally's world than you'd think. It's all there: body modifications, weird theories of beauty, even bubbly-making brain operations.

And every wacky bit of it seemed, to somebody somewhere in history, like a perfectly natural thing to do.

*Certainly nothing is unnatural that is not physically impossible.*
—RICHARD BRINSLEY SHERIDAN

## 1. What are we?

In the Academy of Athens, Plato gave a famous definition of a human: "A featherless biped." Everyone admired that until Diogenes of Sinope tossed a plucked chicken on the ground and said, "See, Plato's human!" Plato quickly changed his definition to "A featherless biped—with broad nails."

For centuries, that answer was as good as any. We had no choice in the matter. We were what nature made us: a mash-up of genetic material provided by a male and a female parent.

But what would we be if we could ignore nature and give ourselves feathers, four legs, or claws? Would we still be human? If what nature gives us is natural, would we become unnatural by changing ourselves? Would we become so different that we should be called nonhuman, ex-human, or formerly human? Might changing ourselves make us so very different that we should be inhuman—monsters whose existence would threaten every natural member of the human race?

These questions are as old as science fiction. In Mary Shelley's *Frankenstein*, Dr. Frankenstein creates a monster that is hideous and inhumanly strong, but in many ways may be more human than its creator. It thinks and loves and feels the pain of rejection. In Robert Louis Stevenson's *Dr. Jekyll and Mr. Hyde*, Jekyll invents a formula that he hopes will turn him into a more perfect human. Instead, he becomes Mr. Hyde, who looks human but whose cruelty and inability to love makes him a greater monster than Frankenstein's creature.

Science fiction asks, "What is natural for humans?" in many ways. What are we if we put our brains in other bodies? If we transfer our minds into computers? If we transform ourselves into alien shapes that can survive on other worlds? Is there any change that we can make to ourselves that should be considered unnatural?

## 2. Uglies

At the start of the Uglies books, Tally Youngblood believes there are two kinds of humans: uglies, who have the bodies and faces that nature gave them, and pretties, who have been improved in every way. To Tally, "natural" means being born an ugly, then becoming a pretty when you turn sixteen. She doesn't expect anyone to care about what nature gives us.

Then she meets Shay, who wants to run away from their city and live in the wild, in the Smoke, with Smokies, humans who decided to keep the bodies that nature gave them. Shay tells Tally, "You've only seen pretty faces your whole life. Your parents, your teachers, everyone over sixteen. But you weren't born expecting that kind of beauty in everyone, all the time. You just got programmed into thinking anything else is ugly."

Tally answers, "It's not programming, it's just a natural reaction. And more important than that, it's fair. In the old days it was all random—some people kind of pretty, most people ugly all their lives. Now everyone's ugly . . . until they're pretty" (*Uglies*).

Tally's upbringing—her "programming"—has shaped what she is capable of understanding. She can't grasp that the point of programming is to mold our idea of what's natural. She can't see that we are all taught what's natural. Studies have shown that human babies born in multiracial communities react the same way to people with dark or light skin—we must be taught to prefer one skin color to another, to think that one is more "natural" than others. How we interpret physical bodies varies from culture to culture. In some societies, fat is pretty; in others, it's ugly. Modern beauty standards call for gleaming white teeth, but not long ago women in Japan, China, and Vietnam blackened their teeth to be more beautiful.

To Tally, wanting to stay ugly is as unnatural as wanting to stay a baby. When she first meets a Smokie, she sees him through the lens of her culture:

"David was hardly a pretty. His smile was crooked, and his forehead too high."

But because he grew up with different values and she is learning to question hers, she sees something else:

"He was an ugly, but he had a nice smile. And his face held a kind of confidence that Tally had never seen in an ugly before" (*Uglies*).

Smokies value what's natural—and by natural they mean the unaltered elements of nature, changed as little as possible to meet basic human needs of food and shelter and healthy living. When David and Tally come to a desert, she asks if it's the Mojave. David shakes his head and says, "This isn't nearly that big, and it isn't natural. We're standing where the white weed started."

That white weed is a constant threat to David's natural world. It's the ecological equivalent of Frankenstein's monster or Mr. Hyde, something powerful and destructive created by men that men could not control, a symbol that says careless change can have terrible consequences.

The white weed is the most obvious sign that the wild of the Smokies is not entirely wild. It has been affected by humans. The Smokies farm. They make buildings and paths. They interact with nature, sometimes changing it, sometimes being changed by it.

Tally encounters a third kind of "natural" human when she meets Andrew Simpson Smith. Andrew's people seem to be simple, tribal creatures who have lost the benefits of technology. They are actually the subjects of an anthropology experiment that has gone on for generations. What seems like the wild is a reservation where tribes of humans live and die without ever knowing what's been done to them. Calling Andrew a savage is simplistic; the true savages are the scientists who observe the people caught in their experiment and never help them. Calling Andrew primitive is equally simplistic; he preserves stories of the past, he understands history and art, and his mind is as open to learning as anyone's. But he is an example of our species in its most natural form, cut off from recorded knowledge, left to survive with what he can find or make from the land.

When he shows his knife to Tally and talks of revenge, she fears him and all he represents:

"here was the natural state of the species, right in front of her. In running from the city, perhaps this was what Tally was running toward."

At that moment, she thinks a natural human is only an uncontrollable killer. But he shows her that our nature includes more than our worst selves:

"Andrew looked up from his knife and sheathed it, spreading his empty hands. 'But not today. Today I will help you find your friends.'"

## 3. Pretties

To be pretty is a common reason we change ourselves. In the mountains between Thailand and Burma, the Kayan women wear heavy neck rings that push down their clavicles and rib cages, making their necks look so long that some people call them "giraffe women." To the Kayans, long-necked women are pretties.

In many cultures, the rules for changing your body are different for men and women. In parts of China before 1911, girls had their feet broken and bound so they would grow up with tiny feet, a painful mutilation that was considered beautiful. In the United States a few decades ago, pierced ears were only for women who wanted to look more feminine, and tattooing was only for men who wanted to look more masculine.

But in some cultures, the rules for pretties of both sexes are the same. Men and women in ancient Egypt both shaved their heads. Baby boys and girls in the Mayan Empire were both bound to cradle boards to elongate their skulls.

The Uglies books give few details about gender differences among pretties. Girls may have modified breasts and hips, and boys may have modified waists and shoulders, but in Tally's city, the reason to become pretty has nothing to do with exaggerating sexual differences. There's no need for that in a world where men and women have equal power. Becoming pretty simply calls for making those sexual differences more attractive.

Or, as Tally might think when *Uglies* begins, "more natural," because in her culture, pretty is natural and ugly is not. Being naturally pretty, however, is unnatural:

"Shay wasn't exactly a freak, but she was hardly a natural-born pretty. There'd only been about ten of those in all of history, after all" (*Uglies*).

A natural-born pretty isn't superior to a science-made pretty—a pretty is a pretty. Being a natural-born pretty might make you a novelty, but it doesn't make you prettier in anyone's eyes. To Tally, how you become a pretty is as irrelevant as it could possibly be.

That changes when she learns that pretties have mysterious lesions on their brains:

> "But they weren't natural?" Tally asked.
> "No. Only post-ops—pretties, I mean—had them," Az said. "No uglies did. They were definitely a result of the operation."

Even when discussing scars on people's brains, Tally's concern about what's natural is limited. She's worried because the lesions are a mystery—whether they're natural is only a clue as to what they are. Until Tally learns otherwise, she's prepared for an innocent answer. She does not assume altering someone's brain is unnatural. After all, it's only another thing humans naturally do.

Most of the ways we modify our brains are temporary. We eat or drink or chew or smoke something that affects our neurochemistry for a few minutes or hours or days, ranging in intensity from a soda drinker's caffeine and sugar buzz to an opium user's high. Seeking an altered mental state is natural for more creatures than just humans; cats love catnip, and many birds and mammals happily eat fermented berries that make them drunk.

One ancient change humans made to their brains was permanent. Around the world, skulls dating to the Neolithic Age have been found with holes drilled in them. The bone around the holes usually shows signs of healing—which means the people survived. Some skulls have many holes, drilled at different times in the person's life.

This hole-drilling, trepanation, has been called the oldest form of surgery. The word comes from the Greek, and means "to drill" or "to bore." Trepanning was done for different reasons in different places: to relieve pressure on the brain when the skull had been damaged, to "free evil spirits," to cure epilepsy. Some people believe trepanning created a constant feeling of euphoria.

If so, it's not unlike the mental state of a pretty who wants to be bubbly all the time.

As a pretty, Tally barely remembers her ugly life. Without an interruption from her past, she would never have questioned her world or her place in it. To a pretty, "natural" only means you have an affinity for something. When Tally fears she won't be voted into the clique called the Crims, Shay assures her, "Anyone who used to hang out with Special Circumstances is a natural Crim."

## 4. Specials

Elongated skulls found in Mayan graves may have been exclusive to the upper class, so anyone could tell at a glance who were the rulers and who were the ruled. Warriors around the world, from Africa to Britain, from the Amazon to Thailand, tattooed themselves to intimidate their enemies. In Tally's city, extreme physical differences is the mark of the Specials, the city's spies, soldiers, and police. They're humans who have been given heightened senses, who were made made stronger and faster than anyone else, who were changed to look superior and frightening.

Specials share the pretties' understanding of what's natural: natural is what you can do or become easily. When Dr. Cable, head of Special Circumstances, recruits the pretty Tally, she says: "'I see you're still tricky even after the operation'—Dr. Cable shook her head—'I realize that you're a natural'" (*Specials*).

Tally becomes one of the Cutters, a group of "special Specials" led by her transformed friend, Shay. Specials like knowing they're special. Shay tells Tally: "How many times do I have to explain this, Tally-wa? You're special now. You shouldn't be mooning over some bubblehead. You're a Cutter, Zane's not—it's as simple as that."

Or, as Tally says, "It doesn't take much convincing to make someone believe they're better than everyone else" (*Specials*).

As a Cutter, Tally never thinks about what's natural until she seeks sanctuary in the city of Diego. When she's asked about her scars by an unseen questioner, she says: "'What, these?' She laughed, running her fingers down the row of cutting scars. 'Where I come from, they're just a fashion statement!'" The voice replies, "Tally, you may not be aware of what has been done to your mind. It may seem natural for you to cut yourself."

If "natural" simply refers to what humans do, self-injury is as natural as wanting to look superior or terrifying. Self-injury takes many forms; the most common is cutting. Most of the world's major religions have sects that celebrate self-hurt through flagellation and other ways of "mortifying the flesh." Some people say they hurt themselves to feel alive. Others say they do it to punish themselves. To Tally the Cutter, self-injury is a natural way to cope with being something that, even by the standards of her city, is not natural.

## 5. Extras

In *Extras*, the focus shifts to another city and another desire that is natural to humans. Like ancient rulers who left carvings about themselves, like graffiti artists who leave their work to tell the world they exist, Aya Fuse yearns to be famous.

Like Tally, Aya doesn't think about what's natural. To her, a "natural body" is only one of many choices. She tells her friend, Miki, "My brother kicked this natural-body clique who never surge. Some of them have to wear these things like sunglasses just to see, even when they're not out in the sun."

Miki responds, "Your brother's famous, isn't he?"

What matters most in Aya's city is fame. If having a "natural body" makes you famous, then a natural body is good—but only so long as it's unusual enough to keep you famous.

Like Tally, Aya thinks "natural" is about affinity, not nature. She tells Frizz, a boy who had his brain changed with "Radical Honesty" surgery so he cannot lie:

> "I think I'm a natural liar," she finally whispered.
> He shook his head. "No, you're not."
> "I am," she hissed. "I can't go ten seconds without slanting the truth."

Lying is on the list of things that humans do naturally. When historians translate ancient writings, the first question they must ask is whether the writer was lying. Plato taught that rulers should lie to their subjects to make them obey. Tally lived in a world built on a lie: the pretty operation actually made people docile. Aya lives in a world built on lies, too.

She learns the secret of the extras, humans who have changed themselves to survive in space. Adaptation is another thing that's natural for humans: from hot deserts to frozen tundra, we adapt to thrive in harsh environments.

At the end of *Extras*, Aya and Frizz make choices that could be interpreted as choosing to be "natural": Aya keeps her big nose, and Frizz undoes his surgery so he can choose to be honest. But they don't question something that would seem very unnatural today: Frizz keeps his "manga face" appearance.

The tension between what's natural and unnatural is clearest in the final scene with Tally and David. She still looks like a wolf-like Special, though doctors could make her look any way she wishes, even like her original ugly self. David is still a natural human, an ugly in the eyes of those who value being pretty. When Tally and David kiss, the two worlds of "natural" and "unnatural" merge.

And they're shown to be irrelevant. Worrying about natural and unnatural misses what matters in the *Uglies* series.

## 6. Postnatural

We are naturally unnatural. If we were not, we would still be eating bugs on the African savanna—or, if you're a literalist Jew or Christian, we would still be naked in Eden.

We have never been content with our natural selves. Before recorded history, we began changing our looks by cutting our hair; tattooing, piercing, and scarring our skin; filing our teeth, binding our feet; elongating our necks; and reshaping our skulls. Modifying ourselves must be a basic human instinct. We do it for social reasons, to identify with a group. We do it for sexual reasons, to be more attractive to people within a group. We do it for spiritual reasons: shaven heads and unshorn hair are ways to show that we've taken a religious path. We change ourselves so naturally that we often fail to notice we are doing it: Conservative Jewish, Christian, and Muslim teachers agree that people should not alter the natural bodies that God gave us—and to show we believe our God-given bodies are perfect, men should be circumcised and women should cover their hair.

When humans developed the ability to change nature, we transcended natural and unnatural—if you think in terms of nature, we're now *post*natural. It's not a word that occurs in the Uglies series, but it's an idea that lies at its heart.

In the first novel, while Tally is still an ugly, David uses "natural" as a word of praise:

"'Don't worry. You're a natural.' He stepped onto his board and held out his hand."

In the next paragraph, something unnatural—flying on a hoverboard—is described as though it were as intimate and natural as dancing or sex:

> Riding double was something Tally had never done before, and she found herself glad she was with David and not just anyone. She stood in front of him, bodies touching, her arms out, his hands around her waist. They negotiated the turns without words, Tally shifting her weight gradually, waiting for David to follow her lead. As they slowly got the hang of it, their bodies began to move together, threading the board down the familiar path as one.

When Tally and David first meet, he is someone she can love, because he understands the truth that her culture does not: "What you do, the way you think, makes you beautiful." His belief that the way she thinks makes her beautiful never wavers even as her body and mind are changed from ugly to pretty to Special. He knows our only natural human traits are thinking and loving and helping whoever we can.

If his faith in her ever faltered, it was strengthened when she healed the damage from the operation that made her pretty. As David's mother explained to him:

> "Your father always suspected that being pretty-minded is simply the natural state for most people. They want to be vapid and lazy and vain"—Maddy glanced at Tally—"and selfish. It only takes a twist to lock in that part of their personalities. He always thought that some people could think their way out of it."

Her comment tells us why Tally is the hero of the Uglies series. An unnatural thing was done to her brain, but she cured herself naturally, by constantly striving to do what was right. Her quest for truth brought her to her final understanding of what's natural for humans: We are what we are.

––––––––––

Will Shetterly's novels include *Dogland*, *Elsewhere*, and *The Gospel of the Knife*, a finalist for the World Fantasy Award. He lives in Tucson, Arizona, with his wife, Emma Bull, and two cats, Toby and Barnabas, who rule them all.

# The S-Word

## *Science in the World of* Uglies

### Jennifer Lynn Barnes

A lot of the Frequently Asked Questions I get about the Uglies books have to do with the science of the series. Could the Rusty oil-eating plague actually happen? Do people really all see the same kinds of beauty? How long until hoverboards are invented?

Uglies is science fiction, of course, so it's no small wonder that science plays a big role in understanding the story. But Jennifer Lynn Barnes (a monkey-studying scientist herself) thinks there's more to it than that.

As she points out here, the series isn't just SF thanks to its futuristic inventions and technology-loving tricksters. Uglies is also about science itself—the ways in which we use scientific authority to manipulate others, and even how our own scientific smarts can lead us to fool ourselves.

IN SCIENCE FICTION, THERE seem to be a few steadfast rules. Governments are evil; conspiracies are common. Nature and technology are diametrically opposed, time travel is a vicious little bugger that will stick it to you the first chance it gets, and—as paradoxical as it might seem—science makes people stupid. Seriously. Given an infinite amount of time, a hundred monkeys with typewriters could produce the works of Shakespeare. Given a couple of decades, four techies locked in a room with scrap metal and computer chips will almost certainly create an army of robotic serial killers intent on destroying the human race. *And nobody will see it coming.*

The world of Uglies, while not completely immune to Four Techies in a Room Syndrome, also shows a subtler and in many ways more realistic depiction of the dangers of science—the kind of danger that has less to do with mad scientists building death rays of doom and more to do with the crazy-alluring, scary-convincing power inherent in the word.

*Science.*

It's the ultimate trump card. You can't argue with it. Most people don't understand it. No need to bother yourself with the particulars—just bow down to its majestic empirical glow. *Oooohhhhh . . . science!* Like a sparkly little bauble (or a fashion-making tattoo flashing in rhythm with your bubbly heart), the word can be a distraction with more surface than substance, made all the more dangerous because in our world—and Tally's—saying that something is scientific is often taken as synonymous with saying that it's true.

For the next few pages, I'll be looking at the roles that science, scientists, and scientific propaganda play in the Uglies series. And I know, I know, some of you are sitting there going, "You could talk about anything you want and you're going to talk about *science*?!" What about David and Zane? What about the desire to be pretty and the ideas implicit in a system in which you can be either pretty or smart, but not both? What about the scary similarities between *Extras* and your own chronic Facebook-dependency? What about kisses and hoverboards and nicknames and slang and kisses (again)?

Well, those are all very important things. Especially the kisses. And the Zane. But in Tally's world, science is power. From *Uglies*, in which Tally believes everything the Powers That Be have ever told her about so-called "biology"; to her discovery of the big neuroscientific secret behind the operation; to the revolutionary world of *Extras*, in which science has been reclaimed by the masses, it seems to be the case that with scientific knowledge comes great power—and, in the immortal words of Uncle Ben, great responsibility. Even the books' premise and the truth behind the operation, taken in isolation, paint a clear picture of the kind of world that awaits those who are content to leave the inner workings of science to the scientists. And that world? It ain't pretty.[1]

Still skeptical? Think on this: Zane's death was completely avoidable. If Tally had thought to ask, or if Maddy had bothered to explain, how the cure worked, he'd still be alive and kicking. But they didn't, and he isn't. And now there is no Zane to fight David for Tally. No Zane to look at Tally from behind seethingly beautiful eyes or kiss her bubbly—and all because there's this idea out there that science is a sacred kind of knowledge, reserved for a specially appointed sect—*scientists*—and best not pursued or questioned by the rest of us.

So, yes. I could write this essay about anything, and I'm choosing to write it about science—and about what happens when scientific knowledge is doled out in bits and pieces by the people in charge. And you should read it. Don't do it for me. Do it for yourself.

Do it for Zane.

---

[1] Pun intended.

## Sugar-Coated Science

"Your nose isn't ugly. I like your eyes, too."

"My eyes? Now you're totally crazy. They're way too close together."

"Who says?"

"Biology says."

—SHAY AND TALLY, *UGLIES*

From our first introduction to Uglyville and New Pretty Town, it's apparent that the government in Tally's city has been messing with its citizens' brains. As an ugly, Tally may not have had the operation, but she's clearly been brainwashed into thinking that ugly and pretty are absolute categories and that ugliness—while a natural state of being—is something to be ashamed of. She's spent her childhood playing with software that allows her to manipulate her facial features, answers to the name Squint, and thinks that mandated plastic surgery is the great social equalizer. And whenever any of these practices or ideas is called into question, Tally turns to her security blanket, the guarantee that she's right and that everything she's been taught her entire life is true.

*Biology.*

When confronted by Shay's reluctance to make morphos of her own face, an invitation to the Smoke, or the most disconcerting claim imaginable—that she, herself, might actually be pretty—Tally clings tight to the idea that science is fact. That biology is irrefutable. That millions of years of evolution can't be wrong. And that—as a result—beauty cannot possibly be in the eye of the beholder.

But what does Tally *really* know? What's being taught in her classes, and what isn't? Is the perception of human beauty really so cut and dry? Or is it possible that science—like history, a quote from your favorite celebrity, or a single line from a controversial book—can be taken out of context to suit someone else's agenda?

Think about the very simplest of all the axioms that Tally considers to be scientific gospel: the idea that there is such a thing as *pretty*, that it's not subjective, and that it's more dependent on our genes than our culture. "There was a certain kind of beauty, a prettiness that everyone could see. . . . A million years of evolution had made it part of the human brain" (*Uglies*). Setting aside the fact that the evolution of the perceptual biases in question probably goes back far more than a million years,[2] Tally's belief that some traits are objectively beautiful does have a good amount of scientific support. In the past few decades, researchers have pinpointed several characteristics that seem to be defined as "pretty" across cultures worldwide. Symmetry is one of them. For women, a 0.7 waist-to-hip ratio seems to be another. In fact, a lot of the traits that Tally identifies as being pretty do seem to have a biological basis.

For example, Tally notes that "[a]verage-looking features are one of the things people look for in faces" (*Uglies*). While it may seem crazy that "average" is *pretty* (after all, what girl dreams of a boy looking deep into her eyes and saying, "You're average"?), several scientific experiments have suggested that this is true! Facial morphing software lets you combine two people's faces and get a face that is halfway between the two as a result. While this can be highly entertaining if you want to see what the lovechild of Britney Spears and Ghandi might look like, it also allows scientists to construct faces that look like the average of *lots* of different faces. Just as Tally would predict based on what she's been taught, the composite faces are reliably rated more attractive than real faces. And the more faces you morph together, the more attractive people rate them.

---

[2] Our liking for symmetry, for example, is shared across a variety of species, many of which share a common ancestor with humans tens or hundreds of millions of years ago.

Other research has shown that when you take babies as young as two months of age—far too young, most scientists argue, to have been influenced by *Vogue* or *Grey's Anatomy* or any cultural depiction of beauty—and show them pictures of faces, the babies prefer to look at the individuals that human adults would call "pretty." If even *babies* recognize prettiness, as well as adults across all cultures, so the argument goes, it must be biological.

Point, Tally.

But just because something has an innate basis doesn't mean, as Tally has been told, that it is completely predetermined, all-powerful, and the same for every person. Science, as a general rule, looks for statistical trends. When scientists say that there are beauty universals, they're not saying that there are things that every person in the world thinks are beautiful. They're saying that, across cultures, people *tend* to think certain things are beautiful. On any question involving beauty perception, the average person might rate something "universally beautiful" as an 8 instead of a 5, but even for the strongest, most consistent data set, there are still going to be people who disagree. Much like there are Smokies and Crims and other people who go against the grain in Tally's world, there are outliers in the vast majority of scientific results. And if you don't see the data yourself, if the people in power—say, your teachers and the evil government officials in charge of brainwashing littlies—just *tell* you that something is true, you miss out on the fact that it's probably *not* true for everyone.

That maybe David really *does* think you're beautiful.

And that maybe he isn't wrong.

An even bigger problem for Tally's understanding of the science of beauty is that, in addition to not getting the full story for any of the individual results she's been spoon-fed over the years, she's also only been exposed to a small subset of research. According to what Tally has been taught, beauty is biological, you can't help but see it, and there's nothing subjective or changeable about it, end of story. And yet consider Tally's reaction to pictures of what are (presumably) *our* celebrities: "Some were grotesquely fat, or weirdly overmuscled, or uncomfortably thin, and almost all of them had wrong, ugly proportions" (*Uglies*). Tally wonders how anyone could find these people beautiful. The answer—that there might be cultural as well as biological factors that impact the perception of beauty—never occurs to her.

After all, science can't be wrong. It's *science*. And the people in charge—the officials and the teachers and the *scientists*—they told it to her!

Of course, what they didn't tell Tally is that there's loads of scientific research out there about aspects of beauty that aren't necessarily universal, and that changing one cultural factor can have a huge impact on what is seen as beautiful and what is not. For example, there is a lot of evidence that there's a universal preference for a 0.7 waist-to-hip ratio. But the most preferred manifestation of that ratio in terms of absolute size—whether you like your women super thin or with a lot of meat on their bones—varies from culture to culture. There *isn't* a biologically programmed ideal for the perfect body. There are only parameters, and culture interacts with those parameters to determine what is really "pretty."

Even the traits that Tally is most sure about being pretty are subject to cultural factors. One of my favorite scientific studies on the effect of culture on perceptions of beauty compares times of economic hardship to times of economic plentitude in the history of the United States by looking at the facial features of the iconic actresses of the times. Actresses with large eyes and round cheeks, who look young and vulnerable (traits that Tally assumes are attractive by biological imperative) are typically more popular when the economic outlook is good and optimistic. In times of hardship, however, the "beauties" tend to have more mature faces, with relatively small

eyes and thin cheeks. When things aren't going so well for us, we
don't want people who look young and vulnerable, like they need
our help. We want people who look strong and confident, like they
could help us! Even in a single country, across the span of a decade,
"pretty" can change.

But of course, if Tally's government-trained teachers had known
to tell her that sometimes the definition of beauty changes, and that
from an evolutionary perspective this makes sense—because in different circumstances certain traits may be more or less desirable
in mates—then Tally might have wondered about the logic behind
what the Powers That Be said was pretty. She might have wondered
if she really was ugly. Worst of all, if she'd doubted her own ugliness,
she might not have wanted to become a pretty in the first place. If
the people in Tally's world knew about the research out there today
suggesting that, while we do judge people based on appearance,
there may be perceptual factors that are *more* important than attractiveness for making split-second judgments. . . . If they knew that
humans are so apt to form in-groups and out-groups that even in the
absence of physical cues like race or gender they are perfectly willing to discriminate based on cues as trivial as t-shirt color. . . .

Well, I imagine there would be a lot more people asking questions about how much sense it makes, scientifically, for everyone to
get plastic surgery when they turn sixteen, and about whether or not
doing so really rids society of inequality and prejudice. A more generous person might consider this a lucky accident. Maybe the people
in charge didn't realize that they were only telling half of the story.
Maybe they weren't hoarding scientific knowledge as a means of
wielding power over the rest of the population. Maybe, deep down,
Dr. Cable is made of lollipops and pixie dust.

But I doubt it.

Hoarding scientific knowledge gives you a certain kind of
power—the kind that allows you to endorse whatever "truth" best

suits your needs. From the perspective of the people in charge, full scientific disclosure would be a nightmare. Far better for them to just legitimize their own views by giving the world a taste of science than to allow the populace to think scientifically about things themselves. If science fiction—and Rusty history—has taught us anything, it's that science is dangerous. In the wrong hands, it can be lethal. As I'm sure Dr. Cable would argue, science is a weapon that can't be trusted to the public. The world really is a much safer place when it's filled with bubbleheads.

## Science in the Hands of the Few

It was a horrible fact to learn.

99% of humanity had had something done to their brains, and only a few people in the world knew exactly what.

—*UGLIES*

Science is dangerous because a tiny bit of scientific knowledge can make us think that we're smart and educated and incontrovertibly correct, when we really only know what we've been told. But in the grand tradition of Four Techies in a Room Syndrome, as previously discussed, science is also dangerous because (at least in literature) there seems to be a direct correlation between scientific advancement and a complete loss of common sense. Throughout the Uglies series, there are ample examples of science making people dumb. While the ultimate and most obvious example is the operation (in which the scientists literally use science to make people dumb), the text is also littered with examples of supposedly intelligent people who become drunk on the power they wield as scientists and start doing very stupid things.

In horror movies, the person who is Too Dumb to Live is marked by their propensity to run into dark alleyways or shady forests with little provocation. In science fiction, by contrast, too often we get the person who is So Smart That They Are Too Dumb to Live—the Dr. Frankensteins and Maggie Walshes and whatever other fictional brain trusts continually decide that the best way to test out a new medical procedure is to inject it willy-nilly into yourself, your children, your spouse, your cousin, and any and all household pets.

The world of Uglies is rife with such characters. There's the Rusty scientist who bred genetically engineered orchids and made them so resistant to threats that they become monster weeds, taking over everything and then dying out, leaving a wasteland that the rangers refer to as "biological zero." Then there's the evil anthropologist who becomes so enamored with his own work and godlike status among Andrew Simpson Smith's people that he has no moral qualms about watching them brutally kill each other—and no recourse when confronted with someone like Tally who isn't part of his little experiment. To a certain extent, the entire Rusty civilization was eradicated because of their dependence on technology: when an invisible plague was causing their machines to spontaneously burst into flames, they tried to drive away from the danger, thereby signing their own death warrants.

To quote Tally, "Boy, you guys were stupid" (*Pretties*).

But the best example of a truly idiotic mad scientist in the Uglies series is, of course, Dr. Cable. Her desire to create Specials, and then specialer Specials, and then even MORE special Specials is pretty much a textbook case. Like many of her fictional predecessors, it never seems to occur to Dr. Cable that her creations might one day turn on her. In fact, Dr. Cable goes so far as to specifically seek out as her subjects people who oppose her at every turn. It takes a very special kind of genius to think that it is a good idea to make one's own enemies faster, stronger, crueler, and harder to defeat than they otherwise would be. Personally, no matter how tempting it might be, I make it a policy not to surgically bestow near invincibility upon the people who would most like to see me dead. Especially when one of those people has already shown that she "resists conditioning well." But hey, that's just me.

Throughout the series, we see Tally in stand-offs against people who've let science go to their heads. Through her own strength of will, Tally beats the operation. She introduces Andrew Simpson Smith to the idea that the world, in addition to being round, extends past the ring of little men that scientists have used to keep him caged. By being wily and willing to risk everything, she uses the cure to take down Dr. Cable. And after doing so, Tally leaves civilization, intent on spending her days protecting the wild from the expansion of the cities—from, I would argue, new science and new technology, and the new stupidity that is bound to come with them.

> "So that's why you're here, Dr. Cable? To blame me for everything?"
> "No. I'm here to let you go."
> "But didn't I, you know, destroy your world?"
> "Yes. But you're the last one, Tally . . . I don't want my work to become extinct."
>
> —TALLY AND DR. CABLE, *SPECIALS*

## Science for All

Thematically, the original Uglies trilogy seems to take a pretty dire view of science. We meet scientist after bogus scientist, and even the "good" scientists, like David's mother, seem for the most part to keep the inner workings of science to themselves (don't make me reference Maddy and the Zane tragedy again). But when we flash forward a few years into the world of *Extras*, things have changed dramatically. According to Aya's appraisal of the world, while it still sucks to be fifteen, the first three years since the end of the bubble-head era have seen an explosion of technological innovations. Aya herself has a hovercam that is "more than just a wedge of circuitry and lifters" and that might, in fact, border on being illegal artificial intelligence. During the course of the book, Moggle is shown to be more of a loyal pet and occasional life-saver than what we might expect from a robot, based on the catastrophic results of most of the science experiments that Tally saw during the course of her adventure.

The very fact that Moggle isn't revealed as the artificial master-mind behind the "City Killers" sets a very different tone for science in Aya's world: all of a sudden, science is fun. Scientists, rather than being those in power, are among the ranks of artists and sports stars, battling it out for a higher face rank. In *Extras*, science has finally gone from being the domain of a small and elite secret society to belonging to the general public. Many of the cliques we meet during the course of the book are *science* cliques. You've got the tech-heads, the NeoFoodies, the algorithm-crashing bombers, tech religion-makers, and people who breed hot pink dogs that spontaneously grow heart-shaped tufts of fur.

Like Dr. Cable, part of me thinks this will end badly (especially the bit with the poodles). There are certainly parts of the book that could easily be followed up with *another* sequel in which science has run absolutely amok—I kept imagining a scenario in which the world had learned the secrets to immortality and some kind of meri-tocracy had arisen to determine who deserves it, and meanwhile, Moggle and his artificially intelligent friends had begun to develop a plan for world domination. But by the end of *Extras*, these dire predictions had not been borne out, and science—in the hands of the people—is shown to be an incredibly good thing. The peaceful *Extras* are colonizing space and preventing the destruction of the earth. They're heroes.

Hovering monkey scientist populace heroes.

Taken together, the original trilogy and *Extras* show a sharp con-trast. Science in the hands of a few individuals is dangerous. It can be used as propaganda, and even the men and women whose job it is to produce scientific knowledge—when that knowledge becomes their possession and theirs alone—can use it to make decisions that have disastrous (not to mention scary) consequences for the world as a whole. But when science is in the hands of the people—when you *know* how the cure works, when you take charge of your own brain, when you have the opportunity to explore it for yourself—things happen.

And as both Tally and Aya discover, those things aren't always the end of the world.

---

Jennifer Lynn Barnes splits her time between writing for teens and graduate school, where she studies developmental and evolutionary psychology. She wrote her first book, *Golden*, when she was nineteen and since then, she's published five other books for teens: *Platinum*, *Tattoo*, *The Squad: Perfect Cover*, *The Squad: Killer Spirit*, and *Fate*.

# Lies and Consequences

*Propaganda in the Prettytime*

## Delia Sherman

Tally begins her adventures with a brain full of slogans: "You can't beat evolution," "The Rusties almost destroyed the world," and "Two weeks of killer sunburn is worth a lifetime of being gorgeous." But very slowly she begins to wonder if some of these mantras might be bogus. And once that happens, the door is open for a world of change.

But here's a question: How did all those slogans get into Tally's head in the first place? And *why* did someone bother to put them there? To answer these puzzlers, Delia Sherman takes us to a history classroom of the post-mind-rain future. So sit down and take out your notebooks, and get ready for Propaganda of the Prettytime 101.

*This tape consists of selections from Professor Hayde's lectures for Lies and Consequences: Propaganda in the Prettytime (Room 46, Level 16). Weeks skipped consisted of class discussions, role-playing exercises, and field trips to the Rusty Museum. Professor Hayde had eighteen students: six ordinary pretties, eight with extreme skin and body surgery, and four naturals who opted to keep their original, unmodified appearance.*

## Week 1: Carrots and Sticks

Welcome to Lies and Consequences: Propaganda in the Prettytime. If you're signed up for Professor Tich's Aesthetics and Body Modifications, it's two levels down in Room 46, Level 14, and you'd better move fast, because Tich takes a very pre-Rusty attitude toward lateness.

You've all been learning world history since you were littlies. And you're probably here because you're really curious about what there is to say about the Pre-Rusties and the Rusties and the Prettytime that you haven't heard a zillion times before. You may think you're going to hear a bunch of new stuff that's too scary or sensitive to tell littlies or new pretties. So I'm going to tell you straight up that it's not going to be like that.

Mostly, it's going to be the same old facts and figures. What we're going to be doing is looking at what you already know in a different way.

Those of you who are leaving, be sure to ping the Scheduling Committee to arrange a new class for this period. Close the door behind you and have a bubbly semester.

Let's get started.

You've all taken enough history and civic studies classes to know roughly how governments work. A ruling body—in our case, the City Council—drafts, discusses, and passes laws and policies that determine all the public aspects of city life, from how many days each year you go to school to who is responsible for cleaning up the streets, and how many new buildings can be built every year.

No government can last for very long or govern effectively without the support of a majority of its citizens. Obviously, most governments try to earn that support by passing sensible laws that keep citizens safe and happy. Inevitably, some of these laws are going to be irritating or inconvenient. The trick is to present them in such a way that people obey them. The presentation is called propaganda.

The word "propaganda" simply means information that is spread. Over the centuries, it has come to mean information presented in such a way that it appeals to your emotions rather than your reason.

The information itself can be true or false. It can encourage people to be kinder to their neighbors or it can encourage them to hate their neighbors. It doesn't have to make logical sense. It just has to *feel* right.

All propaganda appeals to two basic human emotions: the desire for happiness and the fear of harm. Propaganda that appeals to the desire for happiness relies on promises of rewards: carrots. Propaganda that appeals to the fear of harm relies on threats of punishment: sticks.

Here's an example.

Say you're a pre-Rusty living in a little town. One day, a man with a sharp sword and lots of soldiers rides in, kills your ruler, and announces he's the government around here now. If you accept his authority, he'll protect you from other men with swords.

That's a very basic carrot.

If you don't accept him, he'll kill you and burn down your house.

That's a very basic stick.

If he's smart as well as strong and armed, he'll back up these promises with other messages, which balance carrot and stick to encourage you to get behind his policies.

If you accept his rule, you'll be prosperous, well fed, healthy. Carrot.

If you accept his rule, you'll be on the side of Truth, Justice, and Goodness. Carrot.

If you complain about him, everybody will hate you. Stick.

If you disobey his laws, you're helping the guys in the next valley, who are really evil and corrupt and ugly. Stick.

Most propaganda is just a useful tool, like a hammer or nanotech. But like a hammer or nanotech, it can lend itself to bad uses as well as good. Take the hypothetical "guys in the next valley" statement. Propaganda that labels a group of people as evil is called demonizing, and it's dangerous. Once you start thinking of people as evil, you might start thinking that they deserve to suffer or even die. Demonizing can make otherwise reasonable citizens accept horrors like the attacks on the New Smoke and the Diego war.

Nobody wants anything like that to happen again.

This class will help you identify propaganda and see how it works. The theory is that people who recognize when they are being manipulated will be harder to manipulate into doing harmful things.

Some of our classes will be discussion and exercises. Some will be lectures—which are a kind of propaganda, as you will see. History suggests that most people don't mind being manipulated as much as you might think. They just don't like being lied to. When I lecture, I promise I'll try to keep the manipulations positive and transparent. And I won't lie to you. Not on purpose, anyway.

The main text for this class will be *The History of the Mind-Rain*, which is the story of the role Tally Youngblood and her friends played in the ending of the Prettytime. I've pinged it to your feeds, along with some bytes of Prettytime news videos from just before and after the Diego war.

Class dismissed.

## Week 2: Spreading the Word

Today, I'm going to talk a little about how propaganda works.

In the Prettytime, everybody knew that people were better off if they were equal. They also knew that asymmetrical faces were ugly and people with crooked teeth or scars were savages.

Don't laugh. They really believed that. It was as real to them as the Floating Space Stations are to you. Propaganda made it real.

Propaganda doesn't start out trying to get people to believe a lie. Propaganda begins by giving people provable facts, then gradually slipping in comments that look like facts but are actually emotional judgments. For example: it's an historical fact that the Rusties clear-cut virgin forests and strip-mined mountains for fuel. It's an observable fact that they bioengineered species like the white orchids that are still out there endangering the ecosystem. It is not a fact, however, that all Rusties were stupid and greedy and crazy. That's a judgment, just like saying that all people with crooked teeth are savages. Repeated often enough, however, it starts to *feel* like a fact.

As you read *The History of the Mind-Rain*, you'll notice a number of recurring phrases and ideas:

The Rusties almost destroyed the world.

The Rusties were stupid and insane.

You can't change biology.

All pretties are equal. Being pretty makes them equal.

When she was an ugly, Tally repeated these catch-phrases without thinking about what they actually meant. She had no way of knowing that truth is too complicated to fit into a simple, snappy phrase. When Dr. Cable manipulated her into spying on the Smokies, she was all ready to believe that being ugly—as well as burning wood and eating meat—made them as bad as the Rusties.

When Tally had spent some time with the Smokies, however, she learned that living off the wild didn't have to mean destroying it. She met people who weren't pretty, but were intelligent and thoughtful. She learned that looking different didn't have to make people unhappy, and that disagreement didn't necessarily lead to violence and war. As Tally's adventures led her to the pre-Rustyoid villages, the New Smoke, and the city of Diego, she began to realize that her city did not hold the only key to human happiness. She began to question the facts she'd always accepted as true. She questioned authority.

Authority, particularly authority based on manipulation and secrets, doesn't like questions.

Somebody might uncover the real answers and get mad—mad enough, maybe, to rebel against that authority and even overthrow it.

Class dismissed.

## Week 4: The Web of Propaganda

Today, I want to look a little more closely at the kinds of messages governments use to control their citizens and how they work.

Perhaps the oldest and most effective message is a simple appeal to authority, when a government identifies itself with some greater power that everybody accepts as a source of wisdom and truth.

In pre-Rusty days, most lords, kings, emperors, and governors appealed to powerful, invisible superheroes called gods. People believed these gods had created the earth and everything on it. Gods would reward you if you were good and punish you if you were bad, even after you were dead, for ever and ever. Which is like the biggest carrot in the universe rolled up with the biggest stick. So if a ruler could persuade his subjects the gods were behind him, he was set. Soldiers with sharp swords may inspire fear, but divine authority inspires respect.

By the time of the Rusty Crash, the only people who still believed in gods were primitive tribes living pre-Rusty lives in what little wilderness was left in the world. For most Rusties, the ultimate authority had shifted from religion to science. If a government's policies were supported by scientific studies, people were likely to accept them.

The Prettytime built a whole social structure on Rusty scientific research proving that pretty people were happier than ordinary people.

It was more complicated than that, of course. The post-crash scientists reasoned that if everyone was economically, socially, physically, and mentally equal, the world would be a paradise in which all people would be happy and healthy, the earth would be left alone to heal, and war would be unnecessary. Cheap, non-oil-dependent technologies like nanotech and solar-powered magnetic levitation would provide the infrastructure for this brave new world, and the pretty studies would provide the model for a new social order.

Nothing wrong with that, right? Who wouldn't want to be pretty, healthy, and happy with their lives?

The only possible drawback was that the whole plan depended on every single citizen undergoing a major operation on their sixteenth birthday.

The surge itself wasn't much by today's standards—skin rubbed smooth and tight, bones ground and reshaped, teeth straightened and strengthened. But the way you looked, down to your height, the color of your eyes, and the shape of your nose, was controlled by a group of scientists called the Committee for Morphological Standards. And keeping the randomly generated face you'd been born with wasn't even an option.

Of course, the government didn't actually say the pretty operation was compulsory and everybody who didn't have it was a possible threat to society. It just saturated the culture with pro-operation propaganda.

From the time they were littlies, all Prettytimers knew about the pretty studies. They learned about them in school and heard about them from their parents, who were pretties themselves. The benefits of prettiness were everywhere. Pretties lived in beautiful mansions. They got all the bubbly clothes they wanted, not to mention champagne and lobster and chocolate cake. Their lives were one long party, surrounded by friends. Pretties were happy and bubbly and had no responsibilities. Everybody loved them and wanted to protect them.

Before you could be a pretty, though, you had to be an ugly, and that wasn't fun at all.

Uglies lived in a community called Uglyville, in ugly dorms where the recycling holes provided them with ugly uniforms to wear. They were encouraged to play with morphing programs that showed them how pretty they would be after the operation. They attended classes in which they learned about the savage pre-Rusties (who were ugly) and how the Rusties (also ugly) had almost destroyed the world.

Human nature being what it is, the uglies did some of the government's work for it by demonizing themselves. They constantly talked about their physical imperfections and called each other nicknames like Shorty, Nose, Squint, and Skinny. By the time they were sixteen, uglies were insecure, self-hating, angry, and alienated.

And then they had the pretty operation, which turned them, practically overnight, from angry, passionate ugly ducklings into beautiful, happy, smiling swans who didn't care enough about anything to get mad.

Living proof of the Power of Prettiness, right? Propaganda on the nicely manicured hoof?

Well, maybe.

Class dismissed.

## Week 6: When Propaganda Fails

Today, we're going to talk about what happens when promises and threats aren't enough to control a population's behavior.

First, a little history.

After a few generations under the guidance of the Committee for Morphological Standards, everybody over the age of sixteen was as pretty and healthy as statistical analysis and sophisticated surgery could make them. Great strides were being made in the fields of magnetic levitation and nanotechnology, nobody was hungry or sick or cold.

So everybody was happy, right? And there was peace and plenty throughout the world?

Well, not exactly.

Human beings seem to be hard-wired to ask questions and disagree and take risks and break rules. The Prettytime government accepted that some uglies were going to take off their interface rings and sneak into Prettytown or modify their hoverboards. They were uglies, practically Rusties. Being pretty—plus a good solid diet of pro-pretty propaganda—should have taken care of their disobedience. But when the government learned that propaganda can't change human nature, it took a more direct approach to the problem.

Brain surgery.

You all know about the so-called bubblehead operation. It made pretties easily distracted and lazy. It also damped down their creativity, their curiosity, their confidence, and their ability to make decisions. But world peace is worth a little brain damage, right? Especially if nobody knows that's what's happening?

Obviously, everybody couldn't be a bubblehead or society would fall apart. A government needs intelligent, confident people to make decisions and carry them out—to govern, in fact. Occasionally, it even needs strong, aggressive people to deal with physical emergencies. So scientists developed new operations to make people stronger, faster, cooler-headed, and more confident than ordinary bubbleheads. The scientists underwent these operations themselves and they performed a variation on selected rebels to create a kind of super-pretty, called Specials.

Specials were used for Special Circumstances only, Special Circumstances being anything or anybody that, despite propaganda, training, and brain lesions, threatened the stability of Prettytime life. Like uglies running away to join the Smoke. Like Zane and Tally and Shay, whose taste for excitement survived the bubblehead operation almost intact.

Except for troublemakers and misfits, most people never actually saw a Special. They were a scary rumor, like the Rusty bogeyman parents threaten littlies with when they won't go to bed. "If you keep acting up, the Specials will come for you" was halfway between a joke and a threat, shadowy and powerful.

The Specials themselves were anything but shadowy. They were decisive, self-confident, and very aggressive: way beyond cool and all the way to icy. They were programmed to track down anybody who threatened the wild and bring them to justice. They knew they were the good guys, with all the authority of the government and science behind them. Their motto was "We don't want to hurt you, but we will if we have to."

This motto is an interesting piece of propaganda all by itself. It's clearly a threat, but it's a complicated one. The implication is that if a Special hurts you (or even kills you, as they killed Boss when they invaded the Smoke), it's your fault. The Specials are just doing their job, which is to bring you to justice. If you resist, then you are forcing them to hurt you. Which is the worst kind of lie there is—one that makes the victim believe they're responsible for their punishment when the punishment is, by all reasonable standards, unjust or out of proportion.

So the Specials were not only stronger and faster and more aggressive than the pretties, they knew they didn't have to follow the same rules. They were the perfect weapon, and like all weapons, once they'd been created, it was only a matter of time before their creators found an excuse to use them.

Which brings us to one of the worst things a government can do when it feels that its propaganda is failing, that its people are no longer behind it, that its most closely guarded secrets are about to be revealed.

It goes to war.

Class dismissed.

## Week 8: The Propaganda of War

War demands a different, even more emotional kind of propaganda—especially in a population that has been raised to believe that war is wrong. War, after all, was one of the bad things the horrible Rusties did, one of the things that almost destroyed the world.

How do you turn a bad thing into a good one?

You find a really big stick and use it to make people too afraid to think straight: you identify an enemy and then you demonize it.

The way the Diego War began is an excellent example of this technique. After the city Armory turned into a smoking crater, everyone was terrified and mystified. Even the City Council didn't know about Dr. Cable's new, experimental, super-special Specials, the Cutters, or would have believed that a couple of sixteen-year-olds, however crazed, could create such damage. It had to be an enemy, someone who hated the peace and prosperity of the city and wanted to destroy it. Someone demonic. Someone inhuman.

They—or Dr. Cable—chose the Diegans, who allowed extreme body surge, who accepted immigrants from more restrictive cities, who tolerated disagreement with governmental policies.

The propaganda machine was already in place. Scientists are authorities. Dr. Cable was a scientist. Violent people are stupid and evil. The Diegans had attacked the city for no obvious reason. All that was left was to fill the newsfeeds with stories about how awful Diego was, how they'd been encouraging the city's children to run away and join the Smoke, how exciting the attack had been, and how superior in every way we and our city were to the Diegans and their dangerous tolerance of extreme surge and opposing points of view.

Luckily, the war stopped as soon as the Diegan's anti-special serum cured Dr. Cable of her insanity. The negative propaganda stopped, too, and was replaced by positive propaganda, by stories sympathetic to the Diegans and information about reversing the brain damage part of the pretty operation. In fact, it was the beginning of the mind-rain, the beginning of a whole spectrum of new ways of governing, including finding ways of dealing with differences—of opinion, of appearance, even of loyalty—other than simply making them go away.

Which, of course, includes the dissemination of propaganda, both of the carrot ("Being different from each other makes us stronger") and stick ("Only weak governments are afraid of controversy") variety. Governments, like people, prefer to be liked, and can be counted on to tweak the facts, if necessary, to make themselves look good. It's a good thing that our government is encouraging classes like this one, that teach you to see what's being tweaked and why, so you'll notice when things start to get scary.

After all, history tends to repeat itself.

Class dismissed.

## Week 10: Thinking for Yourself

Last class today. It's been a wild ride. The discussion classes in particular have demonstrated, beyond the shadow of a doubt, that you are neither bubbleheads or specials. You're fully individual human beings capable of thinking and deciding for yourselves.

That's what governments are made up of, after all: individuals, each with their own fears and desires, their own demons and dreams. Whether you are ruler or ruled, you're still responsible for recognizing a convenient story when you hear it and making your own decision about it.

Tally, for instance, was not just an exceptionally stubborn young woman with a real gift for getting into trouble. She was someone who did not ignore facts that didn't fit into her worldview. She learned to see that the Smokies might eat meat, but they weren't barbarians, and that the villagers of the wild might carry on blood feuds, but they weren't stupid or crazy. She learned to look at the Rusty Ruins and see human tragedy as well as a lesson in ecology. She learned to work around brain surgery and social conditioning to examine the facts, make her own judgments, and act on them.

She was also self-centered, bossy, and a complete show-off.

So if you start hearing about some particular group of people, how inferior they are, how barbaric, how less than human, remember Tally and Shay and Aya and David and his parents and Andrew Simpson Smith and Zane and the other heroes of the mind-rain. None of them was perfect, not even the pretty ones.

Human beings are complicated and contradictory. Any one of them can be, and often is, stupid *and* smart, destructive *and* creative, sheep-like *and* independent. If you've learned nothing else from this course, I hope you've learned this: However technology changes us and the world we live in, human nature remains human nature. People are people. No matter what they look like, and no matter how far they deviate from what people tell you is normal. Good or evil, harmful or helpful, bubbly or bogus, whatever anybody says, they're as human as you are. Always.

Have a bubbly summer. Class dismissed.

Delia Sherman is the author of many short stories, which have appeared in the Viking young adult anthologies *The Green Man*, *Faery Reel*, and *Coyote Road*. Her novels for younger readers are *Changeling* and *The Magic Mirror of the Mermaid Queen*, set in an alternate, magical New York City. She lives in the real (still magical) New York.

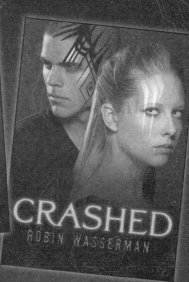